WHEN DID GIFT OF PROPHECY CEASE?

"And if I have the gift of prophecy and I know all mysteries and all knowledge, and if I have all faith so that I can remove mountains, but do not have love, I am nothing." 1 Corinthians 13:2

IS THE GIFT OF PROPHECY FOR TODAY?

WHY IS IT URGENT THAT WE UNDERSTAND NEW TESTAMENT PROPHECY?

F. DAVID FARNELL

IS THE GIFT OF PROPHECY FOR TODAY?

WHY IS IT URGENT THAT WE UNDERSTAND NEW TESTAMENT PROPHECY?

F. David Farnell

Christian Publishing House

Cambridge, Ohio

Copyright © 2019 F. David Farnell

All rights reserved. Except for brief quotations in articles, other publications, book reviews, and blogs, no part of this book may be reproduced in any manner without prior written permission from the publishers. For information, write,

support@christianpublishers.org

Unless otherwise stated, scripture quotations are from New American Standard Bible (NASB) Copyright © 1960, 1962, 1963, 1968, 1971, 1972, 1973, 1975, 1977, 1995 by The Lockman Foundation

IS THE GIFT OF PROPHECY FOR TODAY? WHY IS IT URGENT THAT WE UNDERSTAND NEW TESTAMENT PROPHECY? by F. David Farnell

ISBN-13: 978-1-949586-73-2

ISBN-10: 1-949586-73-1

Table of Contents

CHAPTER 1 The Current Debate about New Testament Prophecy 8

    New Controversy Over the Gift of Prophecy 10

    The Need for A Careful Examination 13

    Prophecy in Church History 13

    Prophecy in the Latter Half of the First Century . 14

    Prophecy in the Second Century 15

    The Montanist Heresy 19

    Prophecy in the Reformation and Post Reformation Periods 26

    Modern Antecedents to the Present Focus on Prophecy 27

CHAPTER 2 "The Gift of Prophecy in the Old and New Testament" 34

    The Promised Revival of the Old Testament Prophetic Gift 35

    Prophetic Personages in the New Testament 39

    Similarity of Vocabulary and Phraseology 41

    The Evaluation of Prophets 43

    Empowered By The Spirit Of God 48

    Concluding Observations 54

CHAPTER 3 "Does the New Testament Teach Two Prophetic Gifts?" 56

    Delineation of Grudem's Hypothesis 57

    Some Weaknesses of Grudem's Hypothesis 59

The Need for Constant Evaluation of New Testament Prophecy 74

Identification of Evaluators 77

The Interruption of Prophecies 79

Apostolic Authority Versus New Testament Prophetic Pronouncements 81

Conclusion 82

CHAPTER 4 "When Will the Gift of Prophecy Cease?" 84

The Miraculous Nature of New Testament Prophecy 84

The Prophet as Spokesperson for the Lord 85

Prophecy and Revelation 86

The Ecstatic State of the Prophet 90

A Comparison of Prophecy to Related Gifts 91

The Prophet and the Teacher 91

The Prophet and the Preacher 93

The Prophet and the Evangelist 94

Arguments for the Cessation of Prophecy 95

The Argument from the Revelatory and Miraculous Nature of Prophecy 103

The Argument from the Analogy of the End of Old Testament Prophecy 107

Conclusion 108

Other Books By This Author 110

CHAPTER 1 The Current Debate about New Testament Prophecy

Spiritual Gifts as a Center of Controversy

Controversy is no stranger to the Christian church. When Paul wrote 1 Corinthians, the first-century church was already embroiled in turmoil over the nature and practice of spiritual gifts. Misconceptions and abuse of the gifts were rampant in the Corinthian church. A three-man delegation (1 Cor. 7:1; 16:17) asked Paul to clarify how gifts such as prophecy, tongues, and knowledge should be exercised (13:8). The outcome of the turbulence in Corinth is unknown, but the second century exhibited the same confusion in the Montanist heresy. The tumult has emerged in the 20th century in and around Pentecostalism, Neopentecostalism, and movements variously labeled "Charismatic," "Vineyard," and "Signs and Wonders."

The gift of tongues (Acts 2:1-13; 1 Cor. 14:2-28) has been the subject of debate for many years. Most recently, however, several books have dealt with the New Testament gift of prophecy. Since the nature and purpose of this gift had not been closely defined by either side of the controversy, this gift has provided a fertile topic as a new phase in the discussion of temporary and permanent spiritual gifts. Questions about the nature of this gift threaten to become if they have not done so already, a major storm center in New Testament theology and church worship.

Among noncharismatics, it has been relatively standard to regard the gift as foundational for the church and temporary in nature. These noncharismatics may be labeled "cessationists." Exemplifying standard cessationist views, Ryrie writes:

> "The gift of prophecy included receiving a message directly from God through special revelation, being guided in declaring it to the people, and having it authenticated in some way by God Himself. The content of that message may have included telling the future (which is what we normally think of as prophesying), but it also included revelation from God concerning the present.
>
> This too was a gift limited in its need and use, for it was needed during the writing of the New Testament and its usefulness ceased when the books were completed. God's message then was contained in written form, and no new revelation was given in addition to the written record."

Charismatics, who may be labeled "noncessationists" (i.e., they deny that any of the spiritual gifts ceased after the first century), generally see prophecy as presently active as it was during the first 70 years after the church began. Kirby, a noncessationist, alleges that the cessationist group, especially those from the dispensationalist camp, has caused much harm to the present belief and practice of spiritual gifts. He says, "Early on, I had a hunch that more had been lost to humanistic enlightenment, dispensationalism, liberal or existential theology, and fear of the loony fringe than we had guessed." By erroneously linking the cessationist beliefs of some dispensationalists with those of existentialism, liberalism, and even the "loony fringe," he illustrates the sharp cleavage that exists between the cessationist and noncessationist camps.

Williams expresses a typical noncessationist stance concerning the nature and present application of the gift of prophecy.

In prophecy God speaks. It is as simple, and profound, and startling as that! What happens in the fellowship is that the word may suddenly be spoken by anyone present, and so, variously, a "Thus says the Lord" breaks forth in the fellowship. It is usually in the first person (though not always), such as "I am with you to bless you . . . " and has the directness of an "I-thou" encounter. It comes not in a "heavenly language," but in the native tongue of the person speaking and with his accustomed inflections, cadences and manners. Indeed, the speech may even be coarse and ungrammatical; it may falter as well as flow-such really does not matter. For in prophecy God uses what He finds, and through frail human instruments the Spirit speaks the Word of the Lord . . . .

Many of us also had convinced ourselves that prophecy ended with the New Testament (despite all the New Testament evidence to the contrary), until through the dynamic thrust of the Holy Spirit prophecy comes alive again. Now we wonder how we could have misread the New Testament for so long.

New Controversy Over the Gift of Prophecy

The recent surge of interest in the prophetic gift has witnessed a crossing of traditional boundaries by some individuals in an apparent attempt to find a mediating position between the two perspectives. Grudem is a prominent example of this tendency. Belonging to the Reformed tradition that is cessationist in background, Grudem has been influenced by the Vineyard movement. He has proposed a compromise between cessationist and noncessationist views.

In this book I am suggesting an understanding of the gift of prophecy which would require a bit of modification in the views of each of these three groups. I am asking that charismatics go on using the gift of prophecy, but that they stop calling it "a word from the Lord"- simply because that label makes it sound exactly like the Bible in authority, and leads to much misunderstanding ...

On the other side, I am asking those in the cessationist camp to give serious thought to the possibility that prophecy in ordinary New Testament churches was not equal to Scripture in authority, but was simply a very human-and sometimes partially mistaken-report of something the Holy Spirit brought to someone's mind. And I am asking that they think again about those arguments for the cessation of certain gifts ...

I should make it very clear at the beginning that I am not saying that the charismatic and cessationist views are mostly wrong. Rather, I think they are both mostly right (in the things they count essential), and I think that an adjustment in how they understand the nature of prophecy (especially its authority) has the potential for bringing about a resolution of this issue which would safeguard items that both sides see as crucial.

By calling for a compromise between cessationists and noncessationists regarding the prophetic and other related gifts, Grudem has stirred up a hornets' nest of discussion on the gifts.

Grudem offers his own new definition of Christian prophecy, one that differs markedly from a traditional understanding. "Prophecy in ordinary New Testament churches was not equal to Scripture in authority but was simply a very human-sometimes partially mistaken-report of something the Holy Spirit brought to someone's mind." In other words, prophecy consists of "telling something God has spontaneously brought to mind." He traces his definition to both cessationists and charismatics. In common with the former, he takes prophecy as noncompetitive with the authority of the canonical New Testament because of the close of the canon at the end of the apostolic era, but he concurs with the charismatic understanding that prophecy preserves "the spontaneous, powerful working of the Holy Spirit, giving 'edification, encouragement, and comfort' which speaks directly to the needs of the moment and causes people to realize that 'truly God is among you' (1 Cor. 14:25)." Consequently, New Testament prophets were "simply reporting in their own words what God would bring to mind, and . . . these prophecies did not have the authority of the words of the Lord." New Testament prophets at Corinth were sometimes accurate and sometimes not. Depending on the circumstances, the prophet could be "mistaken." Only New Testament apostles spoke inspired words.

The words of New Testament prophets were not inspired as were those of Old Testament prophets. This leaves Grudem with two forms of New Testament prophecy: nonauthoritative "congregational" prophecy and authoritative (i.e., apostolic) prophecy. The crucial point of his thesis is that apostles, not New Testament prophets, were the true successors of the Old Testament prophets and spoke like their earlier counterparts with the authority derived from the inspiration of their words. This kind of gift is distinguished from that exercised at Corinth (cf. 1 Cor. 12-14), Thessalonica (1 Thess. 5:19-21), Tyre (Acts 21:4), Ephesus (19:6), and elsewhere (e.g., by Agabus, 11:28; 21:10-11). Only the general content of this secondary prophecy can be vouched for, with allowances made for its being partially mistaken.

The Need for A Careful Examination

A correct view of spiritual gifts is vital, especially since the worship and practice of the church are directly affected by how such gifts are understood. This is also important because of the impact of the "Signs and Wonders" and "Vineyard" movement on some people who have been in the cessationist camp. In view of Paul's warnings in 1 Corinthians 3:10-15 and 2 Corinthians 5:10, it is imperative that Christians develop a biblical understanding of the New Testament prophetic gift. Since this gift has increasingly generated debate within the last decade, the historical and biblical data must be carefully examined in an effort to reach a proper understanding of its nature and duration.

Prophecy in Church History

An attempt at a historical survey of the church's interpretation of the prophetic gift is difficult for several reasons. First, any historical beginning point is relative. Second, the subject of New Testament prophecy has never enjoyed a position of prominence among exegetes until recently. Hill notes,

> New Testament prophecy has never been at the center of scholarly research. Normally it has merited little more than the amount of discussion that is appropriate and necessary in commentaries on certain New Testament books, especially 1 Corinthians and Revelation, and an entry, usually quite brief, in various Bible dictionaries. In recent years, however, the subject has been commanding considerable attention, partly as a result of increasing interest in the investigation of the types and forms of New Testament material and partly as a

consequence of the revival of prophecy in Pentecostal and "charismatic" communities.

Third, some of what can be gleaned about prophecy from the latter third of the first century into the second century A.D. must be determined by inference rather than direct statement. However, church history does reveal how the early church, especially the post-apostolic church, conceived of the nature of New Testament prophecy. This is especially seen in the way in which the early church handled false prophets and the Montanist controversy.

Prophecy in the Latter Half of the First Century

Though Paul sought to halt the abuse of spiritual gifts at Corinth in the middle of the first century, problems still arose regarding prophecy. In the latter third of the first century, the church appeared to be distinctly prophecy-conscious. Since apostles were disappearing, Christians sought for new leadership authority. The Johannine Epistles, which were probably written around the last decade of the first century, attest to widespread prophetic activity in Asia. Accompanying this widespread use of prophecy was a growing wave of false prophecy that increasingly plagued the church ("Many false prophets have gone out into the world," 1 John 4:1). Most likely John was referring here to the secessionist deceivers who were posing a problem for the readers of 1 John. For this reason, John warned his readers to "test the spirits" (1 John 4:1-3) in order to determine the true source of any prophetic activity.

When John's Apocalypse was written, false prophets and false teaching had reached alarming proportions in some areas. In John's messages to the seven churches, the church at Pergamum is singled out (Rev. 2:12-17) as undergoing an assault from the "teaching of Balaam" and the Nicolaitan heresy. The mention of the teaching activity of the prophet Balaam in connection with the Nicolaitan heresy in verses 14-15 gives credence to the view that the novel emphases of the movement were supported by prophetic utterances.

The church at Thyatira was troubled by a woman named Jezebel "who calls herself a prophetess" (Rev. 2:20). The problem at Thyatira was an unhealthy tolerance of her false prophetic activity. Jezebel incited Christians to practice immorality and to sanction the eating of meat previously consecrated to idols. John's commendation of others in Thyatira who had not known "the deep things" of Satan (2:24) may indicate prophetic activity whose source was satanic. The revelations received by this false group were counterparts to the revelations from God received by Christian prophets that enabled them to know the "deep things" of God as in 1 Corinthians 2:10. The situation at Thyatira was the opposite of that at Ephesus, for the Ephesian congregation was commended for its zeal in rejecting false apostles (Rev. 2:2).

As a result of false prophetic activity, opposing ideologies had arisen, all supporting their doctrinal positions with claims to prophetic primacy. John, in Revelation, may have found himself as only one of many competing voices of prophetic authority. Therefore, the warning in Revelation 22:18-19 may be seen as an attempt to settle this prophetic authority crisis. "I testify to everyone who hears the words of the prophecy of this book: if anyone adds to them, God shall add to him the plagues which are written in the book; and if anyone takes away from the words of the book of this prophecy, God shall take away his part from the tree of life and from the holy city, which are written in this book."

Prophecy in the Second Century

In the second century A.D., the tendency toward false prophecy evidenced in the New Testament had increased.

As Friedrich notes, "False prophets caused the early church a good deal of trouble." The result was that the apparently large number of false prophets were not only undermining the authority of true prophets but also were bringing the whole phenomenon of prophetism under suspicion, perhaps aiding in its decline and eventual disappearance.

The problem of false prophecy is indicated in such works as the Didache and the Shepherd of Hermas. They reveal how the early church handled the evaluation of Christian prophets. Though some have attempted to date the Didache around the middle of the first century, it seems most appropriate to locate it between A.D. 70 and 110. In chapters 11-13 the Didache lays down rules for dealing with prophets. Prophets were to be received if their teaching conformed to sound doctrine, but if a prophet remained for more than three days or asked for money, he was to be considered a false prophet. Consistency of doctrine and practice also constituted the mark of a true prophet, for if he did not practice what he preached, then he was to be considered a false prophet.

Similar to Paul's insistence that prophets be examined (1 Cor. 14:29) and John's instruction to test a prophet and his prophecy (1 John 4:1-3), the Didache asserted that prophets were to be tested. A surface reading of the Didache may give the impression that it rejected the testing of a prophet. However, the context of 11.8-12 makes it clear that a prophet was to be tested. The issue in testing seems to be, however, the time of the testing rather than whether a prophet was to be tested. The test for a true prophet is given in 11.8: "Not everyone who speaks forth in the Spirit is a prophet, but only if he has the kind of behavior which the Lord approves. From his behavior, then, will the false prophet and the true prophet be known." A prophet was to be judged on the basis of lack of greed for gain, consistency in doctrine and practice, and demonstration of knowing the ways of God.

Several specific examples of proper behavior expected of a prophet are detailed in the Didache in 11.9-12. If a prophet ordered a meal in the spirit, well and good; but if he ate the meal, then he was a false prophet. If he taught the truth but did not obey it, he was a false prophet. If he asked for money in the spirit, he was not to be listened to unless he asked on behalf of others. Aune summarizes these stipulations by noting that "in short, a Christian prophet must exhibit exemplary behavior." The Didache, in 11.11-12, demonstrated that the prophets could be certified by the communities they served. However, the certification process was not formalized but "consisted of the reputation which the prophet had built up over an undetermined period of time. Prophets who settled in the community were undoubtedly those who had been certified by the community." While prophets were to be examined, that examination need not be continued after an individual had been approved by the community as a genuine prophet. Such rules and regulations may also indicate that the community that produced the Didache was also being troubled by the problem of false prophets. Apparently, some so-called prophets were seeking illegitimately to gain materially from various Christian communities. Thus, as Friedrich notes, the Didache was concerned that "false prophets are abroad and these undermine the authority and repute of true prophets." Unlike false teachers, false prophets were particularly difficult to handle, since they often appealed to divine authority for their pronouncements. The Didache presents basic criteria for evaluating whether a prophet is true or false. His behavior, teaching, and prophetic protocol were to be examined.

Another important work that touches on the practice of prophecy is the Shepherd of Hermas (ca. A.D. 95-115). The Shepherd presents itself as prophetic. It was probably written in Rome (e.g., 1.1, 3; 5.1; 22.2), but its authorship is uncertain. The document consists of a series of divine revelations imparted to a person named Hermas by an old woman and then by an angel in the form of a shepherd. It is from this latter figure that the name of the work is derived.

Mandate 11, one of the more complex sections of the Shepherd, deals almost entirely with the problem of distinguishing true from false prophets. Mandate 11 is unique within the Shepherd, especially since Christian prophets are never mentioned elsewhere in the work. It is a long speech to Hermas by the Shepherd (the angel who functions as revealer) with a few questions interjected by Hermas himself. In 11.1-6, the primary characteristic of the false prophet is that he provided oracular responses to Christians who questioned him on the basis of improper motives, such as greed and lust. Furthermore, a false prophet told what people wanted to hear. In contrast, the Spirit of God speaks spontaneously and not in response to inquiries and cannot be manipulated by man. Aune notes, "For Hermas, the ability to provide oracular responses to inquirers implies control by the prophet over the supernatural power which inspires him (xi. 5); since the Spirit of God is not subject to such human control, it is not he but an evil spirit who speaks through the prophet."

In Mandate 11.7-17, the prophet's behavior is the appropriate basis for judging whether he is true or false. While the true prophet is meek, gentle, and humble, and abstains from all wickedness and evil inclinations, has no interest in possessions or money, and gives no answers when he is consulted, the false prophet exalts himself and wishes to have preeminence; is impudent, impertinent, and talkative; lives in luxury; and takes payment for prophesying. Interestingly a person whose ministry and proclamation centered on wealth or monetary concerns and who claimed to have the prophetic gift was considered a false prophet by the early church and shunned by the Christian community.

The third section, 11.18-21, strongly emphasizes the Spirit which comes from above. Here the Holy Spirit of prophecy is seen as more powerful than the false spirit which comes from below. False prophets infringe on prophetic protocol in three ways: they provide oracular responses to inquiries from clients, they do this privately, and they do it for monetary gain.

In the time of the apostolic fathers there began to be a strong emphasis on heeding apostolic doctrine contained in the New Testament rather than heeding prophetic voices. For instance, Ignatius (ca. A.D. 113) and Polycarp (ca. A.D. 155) both stressed attention to doctrinal truth through the teachings of Jesus and the apostles.

The Montanist Heresy

In the latter half of the second century, the heresy known as Montanism presented a crisis regarding the prophetic gift. This movement began in Phrygia, and by the time it was checked in the church, it had spread to all corners of the Greco-Roman world. The heresy became so acute that even Tertullian was swept away by it. Eusebius, who quoted an unknown opponent of Montanism called "Anonymous," related this account of its origins:

> In Phrygian Mysia there is said to be a village called Ardabau. There they say that a recent convert called Montanus, when Gratus was proconsul in Asia, in the unbounded lust of his soul for leadership gave access to himself to the adversary, became obsessed and suddenly fell into frenzy and convulsions. He began to be ecstatic and to speak and to talk strangely, prophesying contrary to the custom which belongs to the tradition and succession of the church from the beginning. Of those who at that time heard these . . . utterances some were vexed, thinking that he was possessed by a devil

and by a spirit of error, and was disturbing the populace; they rebuked him, and forbade him to speak, remembering the distinction made by the Lord, and his warning to keep watchful guard against the coming false prophets. . . . But by some art, or rather by such an evil scheme of artifice, the devil wrought destruction for the disobedient, and receiving unworthy honors from them stimulated and inflamed their understanding which was already dead to true faith; so that he raised up two more women [who] spoke madly and improperly and strangely.

Participants of this movement called themselves "the new prophesy". It was named after Montanus (A.D. 170), who became a convert to Christianity and lived in Asia Minor. Montanus had been a priest in one of the old Asiatic cults known as Cybele. Claiming the prophetic gift, he was joined by two women, Priscilla and Maximilla, who also prophesied in an ecstatic state. While prophecy as such was not the problem, the sharp departure from accepted biblical norms of prophecy, in content and manner of expression, caused alarm in the church. Montanus and his two prophetesses were characterized by their belief that the trio had received revelations while in an ecstatic state and by their adopting a more rigorous lifestyle than the church demanded.

Neither Montanus nor his immediate followers wrote any treatises, or if they did, none have survived. Fortunately, a number of Montanist oracles have survived in quotations made by early writers. To many in the early church, Montanus's prophecies seemed to convey nothing of any religious or intellectual value. Also, his prophesying seemed to partake of the same irrational, ecstatic prophetic style that was a part of his previous life as a priest of Cybele. For instance, Montanus prophesied, "Behold, man is like a lyre, and I flit about like a plectron; man sleeps, and I awaken him; behold, it is the Lord who changes the hearts of men and gives men a heart." Priscilla prophesied similarly, noting that "purification produces harmony . . . and they see visions, and when they turn their faces downward, they also hear salutary voices, as clear as they are secret." Montanus asserted that Zion or Jerusalem would come down from heaven to either the village of Pepuza or Tymion in Phrygia, and Priscilla's prophesying confirmed this: "Having assumed the form of a woman . . . Christ came to me in a bright robe and put wisdom in me, and revealed to me that his place is holy, and that it is here that Jerusalem will descend from heaven."

Though Montanus's teaching gained many adherents, the early church rejected the Montanists as false prophets. This label of Montanism as the "new prophesy" by its adherents shows why the early church rejected Montanism. It was "new" in that it differed notably from the early church's understanding of the nature of New Testament prophets and prophecy. The criteria used to condemn Montanism show how the prophetic gift was viewed by the early church.

Aune has identified the most important sources in early Christian literature that dealt with the problem of fraudulent prophecy: Matthew 7:15-23; 1 John 4:1-3; Didache 11; Shepherd of Hermas, Mandate 11; and Acts of Thomas 79. From these, he concludes,

> "Two basic types of charges, often combined, were used to discredit prophets regarded as a threat: they were deceivers or they were possessed by evil spirits. The charge that false prophets were mediums through which evil spirits spoke accounted for the fact that both true and false prophets claimed inspiration for their utterances. Prophets who were illegitimate were shown to be such through their behavior, their teaching, and their prophetic protocol."

In the case of Eusebius's witness Anonymous, the Montanists were charged with prophesying in an irrational ecstatic state that was "contrary to the custom related to the tradition and succession of the church from the beginning." In describing the prophetic state of Priscilla and Maximilla, he said that they "spoke in a frenzied manner, unsuitably and abnormally." Anonymous appealed to the example of the Old Testament prophets, whose state of ecstasy did not resemble that of the Montanists' excesses. While true prophets were rational, the Montanists, by their irrational state, demonstrated that they were false prophets. Thus, the early church used Old Testament prophets and prophecy as a model for New Testament prophets and prophecy. If New Testament prophets did not conform to the pattern of Old Testament prophets, they were to be rejected as false. Here the understanding of a direct continuity between Old Testament and New Testament prophets is seen in the early church.

Justin Martyr (A.D. 110-165), the eminent Greek apologist of the second century, also advocated a direct continuity between Old Testament and New Testament prophets. In Dialogue with Trypho 82 he wrote that the prophetic gift of the Old Testament had been transferred to the church. By this statement one may infer that Justin Martyr viewed the New Testament prophetic gift as a direct continuation of the gift as it was practiced in the Old Testament. The same gift of prophecy seen in the Old Testament was transferred to the church with the advent of the Messiah.

Scripture also played an important role in the early church's debate with and condemnation of the Montanists. Montanists identified themselves with Jesus' prophecy in Matthew 23:34, which they used as a basis for identifying their prophets and explaining the hostility of the early church toward them. Anonymous cited Matthew 7:15 to argue that Jesus had warned the early church that false prophets (in this case the Montanists) would seek to pervert the church. He also used Matthew 23:34 as a weapon against the Montanists' association of themselves with this verse.

> Since then they [the Montanists] called us [Anonymous and other opponents of Montanism] murderers of the prophets because we did not receive their chattering prophets for they say that these are those whom the Lord promised to send to the people, let them answer us before God. Is there anyone, good people, of those whose talking began with Montanus and the women, who was persecuted by Jews or killed by the wicked? Not one. Or was there any one of them who was taken and crucified for the name? No, there was not. Or was any one of the women ever scourged in the synagogues of the Jews or stoned? Never anywhere.

Anonymous argued that Matthew 23:34 could not be applied by the Montanists to themselves, for their claims did not fit the precise details of Scripture (1 John 4:1-3). On the basis of their wrong prophetic application of the Scriptures to themselves, Anonymous rejected the Montanists' prophetic claims. False prophets understand and utilize Scripture improperly. Such violations showed that they were false prophets, that is, they were deceivers or were possessed by evil spirits.

Epiphanius, using oral and written sources, advanced criteria similar to those used by Anonymous. He argued that genuine prophets, unlike the Montanists, were in full possession of their understanding and in agreement with the Scriptures. He examined the prophecies of Moses, Isaiah, Ezekiel, and Daniel as proof that biblical prophets were always in control of their faculties of reason and understanding. In direct contrast Montanus's assertion that "Behold, man is like a lyre, and I flit about like a plectron; man sleeps, and I awaken him" exhibits "the words of one who is mentally deranged, and who is not in possession of his understanding, but demonstrates a character different from the Holy Spirit who spoke in the prophets." Again, the Old Testament prophets were a basis for understanding what constituted genuine New Testament prophets. If a self-acclaimed prophet did not conform to the Old Testament standards of a prophet, he was to be rejected. Here again, the early church saw a direct continuity between the Old Testament and New Testament prophets.

Epiphanius presented another important argument the early church used against Montanism: Prophecies of true prophets must be fulfilled exactly. Maximilla had predicted that "after me there will no longer be a prophet, but the end." Priscilla predicted that the New Jerusalem would descend from heaven into Pepuza in Phrygia. However, since the end did not come after Maximilla's death nor did the New Jerusalem descend, Epiphanius concluded that these prophets were false. In the early church any error in a prophecy indicated that a false prophet was prophesying.

The perceived abuse of this "new prophecy" by Montanists led to the gradual discrediting and disappearance of prophecy from the beginning of the third century. Hill confirms this by noting that "the repudiation of Montanism marks the effective end of prophecy in the Church." Although Montanus was orthodox in some teachings, his (and his followers') deviation from apostolic doctrine, their inaccurate and false prophesying, lack of conformity to Old Testament standards of prophecy, and the great excesses of this movement resulted in growing resistance to anyone who claimed to possess the prophetic gift.

In summary, the early post-apostolic church judged the genuineness of New Testament prophets by Old Testament prophetic standards. Prophets in the New

Testament era who were ecstatic made wrong applications of Scripture, or prophesied falsely were considered false prophets because such actions violated Old Testament stipulations regarding what characterized a genuine prophet of God (Deut. 13:1-5; 18:20-22). This idea is reinforced by the belief among some in the early church that the Old Testament prophetic gift had been transferred to the church in light of the coming of Messiah (cf. Acts 2:17-21 and Joel 2:28-30). The early church affirmed the idea of a direct continuity between the Old Testament and New Testament prophets and prophetic standards. Montanism's "newness" as prophecy centered in its sharp departure from norms of prophecy seen in the Old Testament. Becoming alarmed by such a departure, the early church fought against and repudiated it.

One of the first references to the early church's view on the cessation of the prophetic gift is in the Muratorian Fragment, which scholars date around A.D. 170. This work contains the oldest existing list of the canonically recognized books of the New Testament. It refers to both apostles and prophets, stating explicitly that the number of prophets "is complete" and thereby indicating an end to prophetic expression. Heine notes the following regarding the list:

> "It should be noted that the Muratorian canon, which is to be dated at approximately this same time [as the Montanist Controversy] and located at Rome, rejected the Shepherd of Hermas for the same reason that Hippolytus advanced against the Montanist prophecy: it is a recent writing, and prophecy ceased with the apostles. There was, then, at Rome, in the late second and early third century a different attitude toward the possibility of contemporary prophecy than we have seen exhibited in the documents coming from the Montanist controversy a little earlier in Asia."

From the demise of Montanism until the turn of the present century, prophetic phenomena were never a part of a major movement in Christianity. Instead, the focus began to shift to apostolic doctrine and study of the Scriptures as the source of Christian doctrine and knowledge. By the time of Chrysostom (ca. A.D. 347-407) the prophetic gift was considered a past phenomenon. Chysostom stated the following concerning the subject of spiritual gifts in 1 Corinthians 12:1-2 specifically, and chapters 12-14 in general: "This whole place is very obscure: but the obscurity is produced by our ignorance of the facts referred to and by their cessation, being such as then used to occur but now no longer take place. And why do they not happen now? Why look now, the cause too of the obscurity has produced us again another question; namely, why did they then happen, and now do so no more?" Here is a clear statement by a leader of the church in the fourth century that miraculous gifts, like prophecy and tongues, had ceased. Because Chrysostom was well traveled and would most likely have known the general status of the church, he signaled a widespread absence of such gifts in his day.

Prophecy in the Reformation and Post Reformation Periods

During the Reformation, there was an emphasis on returning the knowledge and interpretation of the Scriptures into the hands of the common people. There was also a growing interest in charismatic gifts. Yet it must be stressed that the Reformers themselves viewed "miraculous" spiritual gifts, such as prophecy, tongues, and miracles, as belonging to the apostolic or pre-canonical age, not to their own generation. With minor exceptions, such as some (though certainly not most) of the Anabaptists, the gifts of prophecy and tongues were not exhibited during the Reformation.

In the post-Reformation period, interest in spiritual gifts gradually increased. In isolated occurrences, various groups and individuals claimed to possess spiritual gifts. For Instance, the Quakers, a group founded in England in the 17th century by George Fox (1624-1691), claimed an "inner light" that could be received by everyone. Quakers would sit in silence in their services until God had revealed Himself to someone directly through a form of prophesying. During the persecution of the French Huguenots in the early 1700s in southeastern France, ecstatic experiences including prophesying and tongues-speaking broke out; those involved became known as the Cevenal Prophets. Edward Irving, a dynamic London preacher of the 1830s predicted the immediate return of Christ and a restoration of the extraordinary offices and gifts of the Apostolic Age. As a result of these predictions, he was ousted from the Church of Scotland and formed the Catholic Apostolic Church. Shakers and Mormons also have claimed to possess the New Testament prophetic gift.

Modern Antecedents to the Present Focus on Prophecy

By the end of the 19th century, scholarly interest began to focus on early Christian prophecy. The year 1883 saw a significant turn in research on this phenomenon with publication of Harnack's German translation of Hatch's The Organization of the Early Christian Church. The importance of this was not just in making these lectures available to German scholarship but also in Harnack's own remarks prefaced to the work. Harnack drew out more clearly the implications of Hatch's work, focusing on the prophetic gift.

Even more influential than Harnack's work was the text of the Didache published in 1883, making that year a watershed in modern research on the early church's life and organizational structure. Though portions of the text had been known previously, a complete copy of the Didache was discovered in 1873 by Philotheos Bryennios, metropolitan of Nicodemia. With the publication of the Didache, an unprecedented interest in early Christian prophecy began. Harnack, influenced by Hatch's work and the discovery of the complete text of the Didache, published a text with prolegomena in the series Texte und Untersuchungen zur Geschichte der altchristlichen Literatur. In the prolegomena, Harnack explored the early church's organizational structure, discerning several levels of hierarchy. Harnack's work, however, was derived almost solely from the Didache.

After Harnack's work, other studies on primitive church organization and leadership appeared. Sohm, basing his studies on Harnack's previous ideas, asserted that church authority was charismatic in nature and that any form of law was incompatible with the essential nature of the church. His thesis received harsh criticism from Harnack and more recently from Käsemann for too many generalized and hasty conclusions in relation to the evidence.

In 1921 Bultmann, in his famous work "The History of the Synoptic Tradition", set forth the thesis, based on prophetic and apocalyptic sayings in the New Testament, that the early Christian community used prophecy as a means of reading back into the life of Jesus words that were uttered long after His ascension. More recently Jeremias, echoing this same idea, noted, "Early Christian prophets addressed congregations in words of encouragement, admonition, censure, and promise, using the name of Christ in the first person. Prophetic sayings of this kind found their way into the tradition about Jesus and became fused with the words that he had spoken during his lifetime." Such a hypothesis of radical creativity has been challenged recently by Riesenfeld and Gerhardsson.

In 1927 Fascher did a classic study on the word προφητης from a history-of-religions perspective. Many scholars consider it highly valuable, and it forms the basis of much work done etymologically on the subject of prophecy. Fascher's work consisted of a linguistic and a historical investigation of the Greek term προφητης however, only a small section was devoted to New Testament and early Christian prophecy. In 1929 Streeter produced a valuable work on the primitive church that included an analysis of the information in the Didache regarding the prophetic gift. In 1940 Meyer examined the phenomenon of prophecy in Palestine at the beginning of the Christian era. The main thrust of Meyer's work was applied to Jesus as a prophet and not to prophecy in the early church.

The next round of scholarly work specializing in the New Testament prophetic gift received its impetus in 1947 from Guy's afore-mentioned "New Testament Prophecy: Its Origin and Significance". Guy's treatise provided a basis for subsequent work, culminating in even more prolific activity during the 1970s with Crone's "Early Christian Prophecy"; David Hill's "New Testament Prophecy" (1979); and in the 1980s with David Aune's "Prophecy in Early Christianity and the Ancient Mediterranean World". Perhaps the most recent scholarly impetus to the discussion of prophetic gifts is that of Grudem, whose writings are doing much to stimulate both scholarly and practical questions.

Also, certain church movements in the early 1900s began focusing attention on the exercise of miraculous gifts like prophecy. Contemporary local-church emphasis on its practice may be traced to the foundation of the Pentecostal denominations. Three individuals stand as prominent leaders in the foundation of the modern Pentecostal movement. Richard G. Spurling, a licensed minister, and pastor of a Baptist church in Cokercreek, Tennessee, became dissatisfied with the established churches and formed his own group in 1886. Spurling and Homer Tomlinson, a bishop and general overseer of a Church of God in Queens Village, New York, were instrumental in developing the Church of God denomination.

Another prominent individual in the establishment of the Pentecostal movement was Charles F. Parham (1873-1929), now called "the father of the modern Pentecostal movement." Parham established Bethel Bible College in Topeka, Kansas in 1900. He also developed the Pentecostal viewpoint on what is termed "the baptism of the Holy Ghost." Eventually, Parham's influence spread to California (the Azusa Street Mission), from which the Pentecostal movement and its theology spread rapidly, not only in the United States but also throughout the world. Piepkorn reports that by the later 1970s the Assemblies of God movement had become a major denomination, with approximately 1,300,000 members, and the total number of Pentecostal denominations now reaches more than 130.

At first Pentecostal doctrine was confined mostly to the Pentecostal churches. However, in more recent times what is now known as the Neopentecostal or charismatic movement has swept across traditional denominational boundaries into mainline denominations such as Episcopal, Lutheran, Methodist, Presbyterian, and Roman Catholic churches. The main distinction between the terms "Pentecostal" and "charismatic" is not necessarily theological. While the term "Pentecostal" most often refers to a denominational movement, "charismatic" is a broader term designating those of any denomination who define and accept what they claim to be special works of the Holy Spirit today.

Perhaps the most recent emphasis on the practice of miraculous gifts like New Testament prophecy is in the Vineyard and the Signs and Wonders movements, which have developed in the 1980s. Those associated with this trend affirm the continuation of all miraculous gifts mentioned in the New Testament but then reject the label of "Pentecostal" or "charismatic." Mallone, a proponent of the Vineyard movement, notes:

> "Our backgrounds, both Dispensational and Reformed, taught us to believe that the overt gifts of the Holy Spirit ceased with the apostles. To pass our theological exams we all adopted the party line. After varying lengths of time in pastoral ministry, however, each of us came to the same basic conclusions: (1) the cessation of particular gifts was not taught in Scripture; (2) the church was desperately weak and anemic because of the lack of these gifts; and (3) what we were seeing in our own experience suggested that these gifts were available for the church today."

This movement arose from areas of the church traditionally holding a cessationist view regarding spiritual gifts.

The rise of the Vineyard movement can be traced to C. Peter Wagner, professor of missions at Fuller Theological Seminary, and John Wimber, pastor of the Vineyard Christian Fellowship in Anaheim, California, from whose church the movement derived its name. Wagner admits that originally, he was strongly influenced by dispensationalism and by Benjamin Warfield's theology, causing him to hold a cessationist view on gifts. He notes, "My background is that of a Scofield Bible dispensationalist evangelical. I was taught that gifts of the Spirit were not in operation in our age; they went out with the apostolic church." Eventually, however, Wagner's study of church-growth principles led him to interest in charismatic practices and "forced him to recognize

Pentecostalism as a driving force in much of the growth of the third world."

Formerly a musician, John Wimber converted to Christianity in 1962 and eventually entered full-time ministry. He became dissatisfied with his understanding of spiritual gifts. "I had always avoided Pentecostal and Charismatic Christians ... Also, my judgment of their ministries was colored by a presupposition that charismatic gifts like tongues, prophecy, and healing were not for today (as a dispensationalist, I believed the charismatic gifts ceased at the end of the first century)." Influenced by his wife's joining the charismatic movement, Wimber eventually started the Vineyard Christian Fellowship in Anaheim, California. Though this movement does not label itself as Pentecostal or charismatic, it is similar in belief and practice to those movements. While Wimber's Vineyard church is noted for its emphasis on healing, other charismatic activities are practiced in its worship.

In less than 10 years Wimber's church in Anaheim has grown from a home Bible study of 17 people to a church of over 6,000. Many similar "Vineyard" churches have been formed around the United States and overseas, producing a small denomination. According to Wagner, this Signs and Wonders movement has become so pervasive that he calls it the "third wave" of the Holy Spirit's power in the 20th century. He says the first wave was that of the Pentecostals in the early part of the century, the second wave was the charismatic movement in the midcentury, and the third wave, beginning in 1980, is "a gradual opening of straight-line evangelical churches to the supernatural ministry of the Holy Spirit without the participants becoming either Pentecostals or charismatics."

Conclusion

Blurring of distinctions between cessationist and noncessationist camps has caused concern among cessationists. Sarles wrote, "For the first time in American religious history a noncharismatic segment of conservative evangelicalism has adopted a charismatic view of signs and wonders without accepting the charismatic label. This astounding turn of events has created both confusion of categories and a sense of consternation among noncharismatic evangelicals who are not part of the 'Signs and Wonders movement.'"

The current practice of the prophetic gift has been emphasized especially by the Vineyard and Signs and Wonders movements. Grudem's hypothesis has also directly contributed to the present turmoil regarding the nature and function of prophecy. His assertions about the prophetic gift are now being used as a primary justification of the current practice of prophecy in these church movements. In light of this growing trend, it is necessary to examine the nature and duration of the New Testament prophetic gift in order to deal with this growing confusion about distinctions between the cessationist and noncessationist groups.

The second article in this series will discuss the relationship of New Testament prophecy to Old Testament prophecy. Failure to understand this relationship properly results in a misunderstanding of the nature and function of New Testament prophecy. The third article will focus on Grudem's hypothesis, and the fourth article will address the issue of the cessation of New Testament prophecy.

CHAPTER 2 "The Gift of Prophecy in the Old and New Testament"

Crucial to understanding New Testament prophecy is the direct relationship this gift sustains to Old Testament prophecy. New Testament prophecy did not develop in isolation from the phenomenon of Old Testament prophecy. As noted in the previous article in this series, the post-apostolic early church affirmed the idea of a fundamental continuity between Old and New Testament prophets. Montanism or the "New Prophecy" was labeled a heresy because of its departure from standards of prophecy reflected in the Old Testament. The church judged New Testament prophets on the basis of its understanding of Old Testament prophetic phenomena and requirements. Current novel attempts at redefining the nature of New Testament prophecy (dividing it into two contrasting forms) result from an erroneous assumption of a sharp discontinuity between the New Testament and Old Testament prophecy. An examination of the relationship between the two is needed to understand properly the nature and function of prophecy in the New Testament church era.

That examination finds that the miraculous gift of prophecy operative in the Old Testament economy was the same miraculous gift operative in the New Testament economy. Any differences may be measured by the manner of expression in a theocratic community (Old Testament prophecy) versus the manner of expression in the Christian community (New Testament prophecy). However, such differences do not militate in favor of the existence of any qualitative differences between Old and New Testament prophets and prophecy, especially in their accuracy and authority. This continuity between Old and New Testament prophecy can be demonstrated in a variety of ways in the New Testament. The following are a few examples.

The Promised Revival of the Old Testament Prophetic Gift

During the intertestamental period, Israel as a nation longed for the revival of the prophetic voice of Yahweh. Between the time of the last canonical prophet, Malachi and the advent of the Messiah, in the period known as the "Four Hundred Silent Years," prophecy ceased in Israel. Though claims to the prophetic gift may be seen in the literature of this time, the Jewish people as a whole never accepted them as legitimate. In fact, those claims emphasize the absence of the Spirit of Yahweh from His people and Israel's longing for the promised return of the prophetic gift when God would once again speak. This desire remained intense through those silent years until the silence was shattered by the advent of the Messiah.

The revival of the prophetic gift was promised in Joel 2:28-32. Earlier in that chapter, desolation in the eschatological "day of the Lord" was promised for the nation because of their failure to repent (vv. 1-11). Yahweh pleaded for His disobedient and idolatrous people to return to Him (vv. 12-14). The prophet cried out for the people to gather in a solemn assembly as an act of repentance so that Yahweh would spare them (vv. 15-17). Pity was promised to the people if they would respond to the Lord's instructions (v. 18). Immediate deliverance was promised in Joel's day (vv. 19-27), and Yahweh also proclaimed that His program for Israel had important eschatological implications and blessings. He had not forever rejected His disobedient people, for He would greatly bless them in the future. In the latter half of Joel (2:28-3:21), two important prophetic features are emphasized: the promise of Yahweh's personal provision in the lives of the people (2:28-32); and the prediction of His final triumph on behalf of Israel at the culmination of human history (3:1-21).

In Joel 2:28-32, Yahweh promised Israel that in a future time He would pour out His Spirit in abundance on His people. A spiritual abundance is predicted that would be far greater than any mere physical blessings that could be associated with the promised "latter rains" (vv. 22-26). The Holy Spirit would be given in unparalleled power and ways in the land of Israel. This spiritual restoration and outpouring of Yahweh's Spirit on His people is mentioned frequently in the Old Testament. The same Spirit who empowered the Old Testament prophets is promised once again to return.

However, in light of Joel 2, the Holy Spirit would not be poured out on a select individual or group, as in the Old Testament prophets, but on all believers regardless of their status. This work of the Spirit would bring about spiritual renewal, with the gift of prophecy receiving special emphasis. Because of this promise, the remnant of Israel eagerly and longingly awaited this renewed sign of Yahweh's presence among His people by the revival of the prophetic gift. According to Joel, the same prophetic gift that was empowered by Yahweh's Spirit among the prophets would be restored in even greater measure.

Joel said that the eventual deliverance of the nation of Israel would occur in the period known as the "day of the Lord." The outpouring of the Holy Spirit would accompany this event in "the last days." Later Judaism applied this text to the promise of a renewed heart in the New Covenant (Jer. 31:33) and the dispensing of God's Spirit in future messianic times.

Acts 2:17-21, a strategic passage, quotes Joel 2:28-32. Luke wrote that certain manifestations of the Holy Spirit (speaking in tongues and prophesying) were witnessed by

Jewish onlookers outside the circle of the 120 Christians who had been gathered for prayer on the day of Pentecost. Some outsiders were amazed, while others mocked and said the disciples were "full of sweet wine" (i.e., new wine, Acts 2:13). Empowered by the Holy Spirit, Peter stood and offered an explanation by relating the phenomena being witnessed at Pentecost to the prophecy of Joel 2:28-32.

The phenomena at Pentecost were connected by Peter to the expected messianic times in the "latter days" (Acts 2:17; cf. Joel 2:28). Emphasis on fulfillment is heightened by his use of "the latter days," which brings out the meaning of "afterwards" in the Masoretic and Septuagint texts. As Marshall notes, "Peter regards Joel's prophecy as applying to the last days and claims that his hearers are now living in the last days. God's final act of salvation has begun to take place."

This emphasis on fulfillment is also heightened by Peter's particular focus on the revival of prophesying, which was promised in the Old Testament. He did this by adding the phrase "and they will prophesy" in Acts 2:18 to highlight the restoration of the Old Testament gift of prophecy. Patterson notes,

> The precise applicability of Joel's prophecy to Pentecost can be gleaned from some of the Petrine interpretive changes and additions to Joel's text. Thus, under divine inspiration Peter added to Joel's words relative to the outpouring of the Holy Spirit kai prophteusousin ("and they will prophesy"; cf. Joel 2:29 [3:2 MT] with Acts 2:18). The intent of Joel's prophecy was not only the restoration of prophecy but that such a gift was open to all classes of mankind. The Spirit-empowered words of the apostles on Pentecost were, therefore, evidence of the accuracy of Joel's prediction (They were also a direct

fulfillment of Christ's promise to send the Holy Spirit; see Luke 24:49; John 14:16-18; 15:26-27; 16:7-15; Acts 1:4-5, 8; 2:33).

The solemnity and importance of these words regarding the restoration of the prophetic gift are accentuated by Peter's addition of λεγει ο θεος ("God says") at the beginning of the quotation in Acts 2:17. It is highly significant that Peter tied this beginning of New Testament prophecy with prophetic phenomena of the Old Testament. The word profhteuvw ("to prophesy"), which Peter used in Acts 2:17, is also used in the Septuagint in Joel 3:1 (2:28, Eng.).

By quoting Joel 2:28-32 in Acts 2:17-21, Peter demonstrated that the early church was experiencing an unprecedented outpouring of God's Spirit, which was manifested through the return of the prophetic gift among God's people. This return of prophecy was a direct result of Jesus' ascension and exaltation to the right hand of God as the promised Messiah (Acts 2:33).

In light of this, Joel 2 and Acts 2 establish a fundamental continuity between Old and New Testament prophecy. "Thus, here we have prophecy of the Old Testament type entering into the New Testament era. And this is according to Peter's divinely inspired interpretation of Joel ... This establishes a fundamental continuity linking Old and New Testament prophecy. ... This divinely expected prophetic gift appears in numerous places in Acts, 1 Corinthians, and other New Testament books." New Testament prophets and prophecy stood in direct line with their Old Testament counterparts who proclaimed God's message and will to the people of God. Therefore, New Testament prophecy is fundamentally a development and continuation of Old Testament prophecy.

Prophetic Personages in the New Testament

The direct continuity of Old Testament and New Testament prophets is reinforced through prophetic personages in the New Testament. The Old Testament had predicted the coming of Elijah to prepare the people spiritually for the advent of the Messiah in the era of the New Covenant (Mal. 3:1; 4:4-6). Jesus related John the Baptist directly to the prophecies about the return of Elijah (Matt. 3:3-17; Mark 1:3-8; Luke 3:4-17; cf. Isa. 40:3; Matt. 11:14; 17:12-13; Mark 9:11-14, etc.). Also, Jesus declared that John was the greatest of all the prophets, "thus placing him in line with the Old Testament prophets" (cf. Matt. 11:9-11). John served as the prophetic bridge between the periods of the Old and New Testaments (Luke 16:16).

In striking similarity with the Old Testament prophets (e.g., Isa. 55:7; Ezek. 33:11-15; Hos. 14:1; Joel 2:12), John the Baptist called for repentance on the part of Israel (e.g., Matt. 3:2; Mark 1:4). His ascetic dress was similar to that of Elijah (e.g., 2 Kings 1:8; Matt. 3:4; Mark 1:6), which was the typical garb of Old Testament prophets (Zech. 13:4). John also resembled Elijah by his sudden appearance on the scene, his solitary life, and his uncompromising message.

This continuity between Old Testament and New Testament prophecy is also demonstrated by Agabus. Agabus modeled his prophetic style directly after the Old Testament prophets. As Bruce notes, "The mode of his prophecy is reminiscent of much Old Testament prophecy; it is conveyed in deed as well as in word." This can be seen in several ways. He introduced his prophecy with the formula, "This is what the Holy Spirit says" (Acts 21:11), which closely parallels the Old Testament prophetic formula of "thus says the Lord" so frequently proclaimed by Old Testament prophets (e.g., Isa. 7:7; Ezek. 5:5; Amos 1:3, 6, 11, 13; Obad. 1; Mic. 2:3; Nah. 1:12; Zech. 1:3-4). This same introductory phrase introduces the words of the

Lord Jesus to the seven churches in the Book of Revelation (cf. Rev. 2:1, 8, 12, 18; 3:1, 7, 14). Like many Old Testament prophets, Agabus presented his prophecies through symbolic actions (Acts 21:11; cf. 1 Kings 11:29-40; 22:11; Isa. 20:1-6; Jer. 13:1-11; Ezek. 4:1-17; 5:1-17). Like the Old Testament prophets, Agabus was empowered by the Holy Spirit as the prophetic messenger (Acts 11:28; cf. Num. 11:25-29; 1 Sam. 10:6, 10; 2 Sam. 23:2; Isa. 42:1; 59:21; Zech. 7:12; Neh. 9:30). Like the Old Testament prophets, Agabus's prophecies were accurately fulfilled (Acts 11:27-28; 21:10-11; cf. 28:17).

In the Book of Revelation, the angel who functioned as a revealer to the Apostle John placed him in company with the prophetic line from the Old to the New Testament. In Revelation 22:7-9, John is identified among the prophets by the phrase "your brethren the prophets," and his prophetic power is linked to "the Lord, the God of the spirits of the prophets," the same Source who empowered the prophets of old (v. 6). Though John was an apostle, he is also placed among the line of Old Testament and New Testament prophets, since it was most likely through his possessing the prophetic gift that he was the recipient of divine revelation (vv. 9-10). As Thomas notes, "Since John was a member of the body of Christ and since his prophecy was overwhelmingly similar to the spiritual gift of prophecy . . . John produced this prophecy [the Book of Revelation] through the use of that gift."

Like Old Testament prophets, John used the phrase ταδε λεγει (Rev. 2-3); he reflected a similar vision of the prophetic calling (Rev. 1:9-16; cf. Isa. 6:1-13; Ezek. 1:1-28); he swallowed a small book (Rev. 10:8-11; cf. Ezek. 2:8-3:3); and he measured a temple (Rev. 11:1; cf. Ezek. 40:3-42:20). Geisler aptly summarizes this continuity.

> The Old Testament predicted the prophet John the Baptist (Malachi 3:5). Jesus declared that John was the greatest of the prophets (Matt.

11:11), thus placing him in line with the Old Testament prophets. John the apostle spoke of "the prophecy of this book [of Revelation]" that he wrote (Revelation 22:7). And the angel from God that spoke to him placed him among "the prophets" such as the other "servants" God used in the Old Testament (22:6). And John said of himself, "I am a fellow servant with . . . the prophets" (22:9). So, from John the Baptist to John the apostle, New Testament prophets stood in continuity with Old Testament prophets. And their revelations from God were both authoritative and infallible (see Revelation 22:18-19).

New Testament prophets directly inherited the prophetic vocation of the Old Testament prophets. This strongly suggests that the gift of prophecy in the New Testament was the same as that in the Old Testament.

Similarity of Vocabulary and Phraseology

New Testament terminology is the same when referring to prophets and prophecy, whether from Old or New Testament times. "The early Christian application of the designation profhvth" to individual Christians . . . was originally determined by the prevalent conception of the prophetic role of the Old Testament."

This correspondence is evident throughout the New Testament. Προφητης and its cognates are used in fulfillment formulas in New Testament citations of Old Testament prophets. According to the New Testament writers, the Old Testament prophets proclaimed the very words of Yahweh in their prophecies (Rom. 1:2; Matt. 1:22; 2:15; Acts 3:18, 21; Heb. 1:1). Such prophecies were filled with predictions about Christ (e.g., Matt. 1:23; 2:5-6; Luke 18:31; 24:25-27). Old Testament prophets were seen as writing the very words of the Lord regarding future happenings. According to Peter, such prophets and prophecies were guarded from error by the guidance and inspiration of the Holy Spirit (2 Pet. 1:21).

Προφητης and its cognates refer to early Christian prophets as well. The first instances of New Testament prophecy occur in the Lucan birth narratives. Luke prefaced Zacharias's prophetic declaration with the words, "Zacharias was filled with the Holy Spirit and prophesied" (Luke 1:67). According to this phrase, the basis for Zacharias's benediction was not personal thanksgiving nor a literary product taken from tradition, but a prophecy inspired directly by the Holy Spirit.

Anna is called a προφητις (Luke 2:36). With this appellation, she is accorded a rare recognition in Jewish history, for rabbinic material indicates that only "seven prophetesses have prophesied in Israel. . . . Sarah, Miriam, Deborah, Hannah, Abigail, Huldah, and Esther." Prophetesses functioned in both the Old and New Testaments (Exod. 15:20; Judg. 4:4; 2 Kings 22:14; Neh. 6:14; Isa. 8:3; Acts 2:17; 21:9; 1 Cor. 11:5). Anna seems to have been called a prophetess because of her gift of foreseeing future events (Luke 2:38).

The Jews and Jesus considered John the Baptist to be a prophet (Matt. 11:9-14; Luke 20:6). The people of Palestine thought Jesus was a prophet (Matt. 16:14; 21:46). Some recognized Him as the fulfillment of the promised great prophet of Deuteronomy 18:15 (John 6:14; 7:40; cf. Acts 3:19-22). The Jews also believed that the test of a true prophet included the miraculous ability to prophesy accurately and correctly even under difficult circumstances (e.g., Matt. 26:67-68; Luke 7:16, 39; 9:8, 19; John 4:19).

Also, προφητης and its cognates are used to refer to contemporary New Testament prophets in the church (Acts 11:27-30; 15:32; 21:10-11; 1 Cor. 12-14; Eph. 2:20; 3:5-10; 4:11; Rev. 22:6-10). Clearly, the New Testament makes no distinctions in vocabulary or phraseology between references to Old and New Testament prophecy or prophets.

The Evaluation of Prophets

In the Old Testament, those who claimed to have the prophetic gift were to be evaluated by the people of Israel to determine whether they and their prophecies were legitimate. The Old Testament gives important principles for distinguishing between acceptable and unacceptable prophets and prophecies.

Deuteronomy 13:1-13 and 18:20-22 are major passages dealing with the question of true and false prophets. Any so-called prophet who enticed the nation or individual Israelites to worship a god other than Yahweh was to be removed from the community by the severest penalty, namely, death (13:5). The reaction Israel exhibited toward false prophets was viewed as a test to determine whether they desired to follow and love Him exclusively (13:3).

Any prophet who spoke presumptuously or falsely in Yahweh's name but had not been genuinely called to that office or inspired by His Spirit was to be put to death (Deut. 18:20-22). A sign of a true prophet was that his prophecies actually came true, implying that if Yahweh was behind the prophetic commission, He would not let His words spoken through the prophet fail.

The Old Testament frequently emphasized the requirement of accuracy for verifying a true prophet. Since a genuine prophet was empowered by Yahweh's Spirit, any deviation from truth or accuracy would be a sign of a false prophet. False prophets were to be summarily rejected by the nation. The one who spoke presumptuously was to be distinguished from the one who spoke through the Spirit of the Lord. And the true prophet was to be distinguished from the false prophet on the basis of whether his proclamations were true or false.

Yet even if the prophet's words came true, this did not necessarily mean he was a genuine prophet (Deut. 13:1-4). False prophets could sometimes feign true prophecies. The source of the prophecy had to be determined. Was it genuinely from God, or from the imagination of the false prophet ("spoken presumptuously," Deut. 18:22), or even demonic (1 Kings 22:20-21; 2 Chron. 18:19-22)?

Even a true prophet could apostasize and declare something that was not truly from Yahweh's Spirit (1 Kings 13:11-25). Therefore, continued vigilance and constant evaluation of every prophet's words were needed. The difference between a genuine and a false prophet could be determined only by careful examination of the prophet's life and message in accord with the written Word of Yahweh (Deut. 13:4, 18). The reputation of the true prophet could be established only over a period of time.

No tolerance of a false prophet or prophecy was to be allowed, as seen by the severe penalty of death for such an infraction (Deut. 13:5; 18:20). This was so severe because someone who spoke as a prophet in Yahweh's name was claiming the high honor of being Yahweh's spokesman who had direct contact with Him. As such a representative, the prophet could demand obedience from his hearers. False prophets could potentially do much damage to the theocratic community in leading the people astray from Yahweh.

These rules in Deuteronomy 13:1-13 and 18:20-22 were applicable even to established prophets like Samuel and Isaiah. Even if an Old Testament prophet gained a reputation so that he may not have been formally or constantly evaluated, he was still subject to the background requirements of Deuteronomy 13 and 18. At the very least, the stated requirements served to reinforce the genuineness of the true prophet, because a true prophet must accurately proclaim the truth (e.g., 1 Sam. 3:19).

Sadly, Old Testament prophets often became revered only by later generations. Frequently Israel failed to expose false prophets while persecuting Yahweh's true prophets (e.g., 1 Kings 19:10; Jer. 37:1-21). Only as later generations realized that their ancestors had been disobedient idolaters who failed to recognize the prophets' advice (cf. Ezra 9:1-15; Neh. 9:30-31; Dan. 9:6) did the prophets ascend to a place of esteem. This latter thought was reinforced by Jesus when He recalled that Israel had consistently despised, rejected, and killed her prophets: "O Jerusalem, Jerusalem, who kills the prophets and stones those who are sent to her" (Matt. 23:37).

The apostles, being Jews who were keenly aware of the Old Testament, remembered the admonitions to evaluate those who claimed to have the prophetic gift. The New Testament furnishes no indication that the Jews in that day, particularly those who became apostles in the early church, considered the requirements for prophets to have been abrogated or substantially modified. Just as evaluation was needed in the Old Testament to determine genuine prophets from false prophets so evaluation was needed in the New Testament.

The critical need for evaluating New Testament prophets should also be understood in light of Jesus' warning in Matthew 24:11. "Many false prophets," He said, would arise and deceive people.

In light of the promised return of prophecy, as seen in Joel 2:28-32 and Acts 2:17-21, the prophetic Holy Spirit had been poured out on the people of God once again. While not all in the New Testament era could claim the prophetic gift (because of God's sovereign distribution of spiritual gifts; 1 Cor. 12:4-31, esp. v. 29), a much larger group of potential prophets became possible because of the special outpouring of the Holy Spirit on the day of Pentecost ("I will pour forth of My Spirit upon all mankind; and your sons and your daughters shall prophesy," Acts 2:17; cf. Joel 2:28).

With a larger number of genuine prophets, the potential for false prophets and prophecies increased. This expanded sphere of prophetic activity increased the need for care in discerning true prophets from false prophets. As noted in the previous article in this series, the early church struggled with a growing wave of false prophecy, especially during the latter half of the first century. "Many false prophets have gone out into the world" (1 John 4:1; cf. 2 Pet. 2:1-3; 2 John 10-11; 3 John 9-10; Jude 8-23). Such false prophesying, with its accompanying false profession, would have created confusion and uncertainty in some areas of the church regarding the truths of Christianity. Eventually, this wave of false prophecy led in the second century A.D. to the prophetic crisis known as Montanism.

The marked increase in the number of prophets caused the early church to exhibit a cautious attitude in accepting the prophecies of those claiming the prophetic gift. Need for caution is especially seen during the period of the formation of the doctrine of the first-century church. Such care is also evident by the fact that, along with apostles, New Testament prophets served a vitally important role in the foundation of the early church, according to Ephesians 2:20. Through the apostles and New Testament prophets, the first-century church received its revelatory/doctrinal information and guidance (cf. Eph. 3:5-10; 4:7-16) so that the church could reach maturity and understanding in the faith (4:12-14).

Paul's stipulations in 1 Corinthians 12-14 for evaluating prophets and their prophecies were based on Old Testament admonitions for such evaluation, Jesus' warning about false prophets, and the increased number of potential prophets. Just as the Old Testament prophets were to be examined, so too the New Testament prophets were to be evaluated.

The increased potential for false prophets created the need Paul attempted to meet in 1 Corinthians 14:29-31. The larger the group of prophets, the more potential there was for the abuse of prophecy by those who were not New Testament prophets. Just as false prophets of old opposed the divinely chosen leaders and spokesmen (prophets) of Yahweh in ancient Israel, so false prophets and teachers challenged apostolic authority and doctrine (Gal. 2:4-5; 2 Tim. 2:18; Jude 3). Such false prophetic activity in the early church pointed up the need to heed the Old Testament admonition to evaluate prophets. Just as the Old Testament commanded the theocratic community to evaluate all alleged Old Testament prophets, so Paul gave the Christian community a corresponding admonition to evaluate all so-called New Testament prophets. As Saucy remarks, "Some evaluation of the content of Old Testament prophecy was required even as Paul instructed in the church. To be sure with the increase of prophetic activity in the church with the coming of the Spirit under the new covenant, evaluations might be more frequent. But the principle does not appear to be different than that in the Old Testament."

First Corinthians 12:1-3 sheds additional light on the situation addressed in 1 Corinthians 14:29. Apparently, false prophets had preached that Jesus was "accursed" (12:3) even though they professed to be true prophets. The person making such a startling statement must have been a professed Christian. Otherwise, his statement would not have been tolerated in a Christian assembly and would not have been attributed to the Holy Spirit, as apparently claimed ("No one speaking by the Spirit of God says, 'Jesus is accursed,'" v. 3). In the face of such starkly erroneous prophesying, Paul warned the congregation to evaluate each prophecy carefully to ensure that a genuine prophet was speaking. Some recognized voice was needed to declare that the Holy Spirit was not the source of such a statement and that the person voicing it was a false prophet. First Corinthians 14:29 does not necessarily mean that established prophets had to be verified continually. Yet the general rule that any potential prophet needed to be scrutinized by other prophets is stipulated. The evaluative process laid down by Paul emphasizes the need for careful analysis of any prophet who claimed to speak by the Spirit of God. According to 2 Corinthians 11:13-15, even false prophets had potential to feign a true prophecy (cf. Deut. 13:2). So, Paul encouraged a continued vigil. The regular ministry of prophets was to ensure the genuineness of prophets and prophecies as a safeguard against doctrinal heresies.

Paul also laid down the guideline that genuine prophets and prophecy are to be in agreement with apostolic doctrine. Since apostolic doctrine and true prophets have their source in God, one evidence that a prophecy was genuine would be its agreement with apostolic truth (1 Cor. 14:37-38; cf. Gal. 1:8-9). While false prophets challenged apostolic authority, the true prophet would recognize Paul's words and commandments as coming directly from the Lord Jesus Christ. Any alleged prophet opposing apostolic standards and elevating himself to the role of God's only spokesman (1 Cor. 14:36) was to be recognized as false and his authority rejected (v. 38).

In summary, the early church, in evaluating prophets, was heeding the warning of both the Old Testament and Jesus. Such a careful evaluation also reflected the increased sphere of prophetic activity in the New Testament era.

Empowered By The Spirit Of God

Prophets in both the Old and New Testaments were empowered by the Holy Spirit in the exercise of their gift. An intimate relationship existed between the Holy Spirit and the prophet of God. Old Testament prophets prophesied as a direct result of the empowerment and influence of the Spirit of Yahweh (see, e.g., Zech. 7:12). The Spirit of Yahweh is the Spirit of prophecy (see, e.g., Neh. 9:30).

According to Peter, the Holy Spirit was the Source of the prophet's inspiration: "No prophecy was ever made by an act of human will, but men moved by the Holy Spirit spoke from God" (2 Pet. 1:21). As such, the Holy Spirit also guaranteed the accuracy of the prophecies because He was the prime Motivator of the prophet (2 Pet. 1:19; 2 Tim. 3:16). Because the Holy Spirit guided and guarded the men involved in giving prophecies, these predictions were accurate down to the very words (Matt. 5:18; John 10:35; 2 Tim. 3:16).

The Holy Spirit's empowering of prophets continued into the New Testament era. The coming of the prophetic gift on the day of Pentecost in Acts 2:17-21 was a direct result of the outpouring of the Holy Spirit of prophecy ("I will pour forth of My Spirit upon all mankind, and your sons and your daughters shall prophecy"). The prophet Agabus predicted a coming famine through the agency of the Holy Spirit and, as a result, the prophecy was accurately fulfilled (Acts 11:28). Again Agabus, empowered by the Holy Spirit, warned Paul about his fate if he should enter Jerusalem (21:11). His prophecy was accurately fulfilled (21:27-22:29; 28:17).

In addressing the abuse of the spiritual gift of prophecy in 1 Corinthians 12:3, Paul stressed that "no one speaking by the Spirit of God says, 'Jesus is accursed.'" No one who prophesies under the power of the Holy Spirit will issue such erroneous prophecy. The Holy Spirit is the one who guards genuine prophecies. This is in keeping with the Old Testament teaching that a prophet was considered false if his prophecies did not come true (Deut.

18:22) or if they led away from worship of the Lord (13:1-2).

Paul made known that early church prophets, along with the apostles, received the important revelation of Gentile inclusion in the church (Eph. 3:5-10). This revelation came through the Holy Spirit.

In 1 John 4:1-3, Christians are urged to "test" the source behind the prophet to determine whether the source is from God or is demonically influenced (v. 3). According to John, the true prophet brings forth genuine prophecy which has its source in God, while the sign of a false prophet is false prophecy. Again, the Old Testament admonition to test prophets is reflected.

The Holy Spirit maintained an intimate relationship with prophecy in both the Old and New Testament economies. Because the Holy Spirit is the Source behind the prophet of God in both, the Spirit serves as the sovereign Guardian of the accuracy of prophecies from God (cf. Heb. 6:18).

Prophetic Voice for the Community

Prophets in the Old Testament served as the voice of Yahweh to the theocratic community of Israel. They were recipients of revelations directly from Yahweh, which revelations they proclaimed to the nation (Isa. 6:8-13; Jer. 1:5-10; Ezek. 2:1-10).

Just as the Old Testament prophets served as the prophetic voice of communication and instruction from Yahweh, so New Testament prophets functioned in the same capacity. Ephesians 2:20 points out that New Testament prophets too functioned as prophetic voices for the believing community. However, this verse is not without interpretive problems.

In the phrase "foundation of the apostles and prophets", does the word "prophets" refer to prophets of the Old Testament or the New Testament? Some commentators say it refers to the Old Testament prophets. Two arguments are usually cited in support of this view. (1) The New Testament apostles added their testimonies to that of the Old Testament prophets in the revelation they transmitted concerning Christ. (2) The metaphor of a building foundation suggests that Gentiles are now being added to Old Testament Jews, as part of the same spiritual building. A similar metaphor is seen in Romans 11:17-24.

Other commentators understand "prophets" to refer to New Testament prophets. Certain arguments militate against the former view and support the view of New Testament prophets. (1) The word "apostles" comes before "prophets." If Old Testament prophets were in view, "prophets" should have preceded "apostles". (2) Ephesians 3:5 relates that the mystery of Gentile inclusion was not previously made known as it has now been made known ("to His holy apostles and prophets"). The prophets are clearly perceived as the inspired contemporaries of the apostles, enjoying similar revelations of truth from the same Holy Spirit. This mystery was not revealed to Old Testament prophets, for it is only "now" in the Church Age that this mystery has been revealed (3:10; Col. 1:26). The nuvn in Ephesians 3:10 and Colossians 1:26 marks a contrast between the two ages. This mystery was unknown to former generations, but it is now revealed to the apostles and New Testament prophets. (3) The phrase in Ephesians 4:11 that Christ gave "some apostles and some prophets" also supports the view that New Testament prophets are meant in 2:20 and 3:5. In Ephesians 4:11 the New Testament prophets are seen as a special class who ranked next to the apostles. (4) The context of Ephesians 2:20 also favors the view that New Testament prophets are meant. If Old Testament prophets were meant, it is difficult to account for Christ being the Cornerstone, that is, the first stone laid in the foundation. Christ, as the New Covenant Mediator, is in view in verses 14-18, and He came in that role long after the Old Testament prophets. The fact that a cornerstone of a building is laid before any other stones suggests the chronological order of first, Jesus, then the apostles, and then New Testament prophets. (5) The "new man," a reference to the uniting of Jew and Gentile into one body, the church, is completely distinct from the old order, which entailed enmity between Jews and Gentiles because of the Law (Eph. 2:15).

Hence it seems probable that "prophets" refers to New Testament prophets. They, along with the apostles, received the revelation of the mystery of the church in the present age, which had been hidden in days past (Eph. 3:5; 4:11).

Another important issue pertaining to Ephesians 2:20 is how the phrase "of the apostles and prophets" modifies "foundation." Is it a subjective genitive, "the foundation which has been laid by the apostles and prophets," or is it an appositional genitive, "the foundation which consists of the apostles and prophets"? In the first view "foundation" refers not to the apostles and prophets themselves, but to their preaching and teaching, or their activity of receiving and proclaiming the gospel, or their ruling and guiding activity in the New Testament church.

However, the following may be noted in response to the first view. (1) The wording in Ephesians 2:20 requires that the building consists entirely of persons. This can be seen by the fact that the plural participle "having been built upon" most naturally refers, not to the house which is built, but to "you" as implied by εστε ("you are") in the previous verse (v. 19). Thus the Gentile converts are added to the foundation of the apostles and prophets. This can be further demonstrated by the fact that Christ is best understood as the chief "cornerstone," the primary Stone of the foundation. Therefore, the metaphor in Ephesians 2:20 points to components of the dwelling place of God (v. 22): the Gentiles, the Jewish apostles and New

Testament prophets, and Christ. All these elements are individuals who are joined together in a new house.

(2) The metaphor of a living, growing house (v. 21) in which God dwells (v. 22) fits with a picture of a house consisting of persons, but it fits poorly with the picture of a house having components that are impersonal teachings or activities (cf. 1 Pet. 2:4-8). No explicit mention is made in the context of teaching activity or Christian doctrine or any other impersonal factor.

(3) Passages cited as parallels to Ephesians 2:20 do not actually support the view that the foundation is laid by the apostles and prophets (viz., 1 Cor. 3:10-11; Rom. 15:20), for they are not true parallels. In 1 Corinthians 3:10-11, Paul stated directly that he laid the foundation, but in Ephesians 2:20 he did not say this. First Corinthians 3 discusses building works on the foundation (Christ) in light of the Judgment Seat, whereas Ephesians 2 contains no mention of building works on a foundation. The foundation in Romans 15:20 is that of developing new local churches, but in Ephesians 2:20 the universal church is in view.

The second major view of the genitive phrase in Ephesians 2:20 is that it is appositional, that is, the foundation consists of the apostles and New Testament prophets. This seems to be the more natural interpretation, for it fits well in the immediate context of 2:19-21. As stated earlier, persons are in view in the formation of the building: the Gentiles, the apostles and prophets, and Christ. Here the metaphor expresses the fact that the church's foundation, the apostles and New Testament prophets, needed to be correctly aligned with Christ, the chief Cornerstone. This view also makes sense in the context of Ephesians 4:11, where the apostles and New Testament prophets are seen as gifted men given to the church as its "foundation" (cf. 1 Cor. 12:28).

Ephesians 2:20, then, points to the strategic, foundational role played by New Testament prophets in the formation of the church. The prophets, in association with the apostles, held the important status of helping lay the church's foundation. This would indicate the high degree of prestige enjoyed by New Testament prophets in the Christian community. Their ranking in the list of gifted persons in 1 Corinthians 12:28 places them second only to the apostles in usefulness to the body of Christ. Moreover, Paul urged his readers to desire prophecy above the other gifts (cf. 1 Cor. 14:1).

While several apostles received divine revelation (e.g., Paul, John, and Peter), New Testament prophets also received revelation and gave immediate and temporal advice to local congregations. That is, many New Testament prophets gave oral rather than canonical revelation. Since, however, such canonical books as Luke-Acts, Mark, and Hebrews (Heb. 2:3-4) were written by nonapostles and their books were canonically received, most likely the New Testament prophetic gift was involved in their composition. Apostles also probably received their inspired and authoritative revelations through exercising of the same prophetic gift exhibited by New Testament prophets like Agabus.

Much as Old Testament prophets functioned as the prophetic voice in the theocratic community, receiving direct revelations, so apostles and New Testament prophets were vitally involved in the formative, revelatory period of the early church. Prophets were vehicles for revelation from God and held a high profile among early Christians for this reason.

Concluding Observations

The fundamental continuity of the Old Testament and New Testament prophecy was demonstrated in several ways in the New Testament. As such, it stands in direct contradiction to recent attempts to bifurcate the New Testament prophetic gift into two distinct forms such as authoritative apostolic prophecy and nonauthoritative congregational prophecy. The case for nonauthoritative "congregational" prophecy in 1 Corinthians 12-14 and elsewhere in Scripture incorrectly posits a strong discontinuity between Old Testament and New Testament prophecy. Such a view does injustice to the fact that New Testament prophecy is founded on and has a significant continuity with the Old Testament prophetic phenomena and experience. Such a dichotomy also results in the assertion that New Testament prophecy contained fallible revelation, which in itself is a contradiction in terms. In light of this, the third article in this series will deal with the hypothesis of Wayne Grudem, who offers the most current attempt at justifying two forms of New Testament prophecy.

CHAPTER 3 "Does the New Testament Teach Two Prophetic Gifts?"

In the second century, post-apostolic Christianity faced a serious challenge from the prophetic crisis known as the "New Prophecy" (nea profhteia) or Montanism. This labeling of Montanism as the "New Prophecy" by its adherents shows why the early church rejected Montanism: it was "new" in that it differed markedly from the early church's understanding of the nature of New Testament prophets and prophecy. As noted, this understanding by the early church came from the standards set by the Old Testament for the evaluation of prophets. Before being checked, Montanism spread rapidly throughout the Greco-Roman world and quickly won many adherents, so that even the church father Tertullian was swept away by its claims. Such a sharp departure from accepted biblical norms of prophecy, especially in its content and manner of expression, caused great alarm. The crisis became so acute that the church struggled for decades to quell the swelling numbers of adherents to Montanism.

Now in the 20th century, Christianity is once again facing a prophetic crisis. Its original impetus occurred in the Pentecostal and charismatic movements, which developed in the late 19th and early 20th centuries. Recently, however, the momentum has come from the Vineyard and the Signs and Wonders movements, which have spread rapidly among churches that have held traditionally to the "cessationist" viewpoint regarding New Testament prophecy. These groups essentially argue that prophets and prophecy are active today as they were in the first-century church.

Defense of this practice of "prophecy" has recently come from the work of Wayne A. Grudem, who is active in a Vineyard-affiliated church and is an associate professor of biblical and systematic theology at Trinity Evangelical Divinity School in Deerfield, Illinois. Grudem's arguments have become a primary justification for this form of "prophecy" not only in Vineyard fellowships but also among such groups as the Signs and Wonders movement and the Kansas City Fellowship of prophets. Accolades for his view are coming from within and without the charismatic and Pentecostal movements, while some express hope that this work could be used as a means of fostering dialogue between cessationists and noncessationists.

Since Grudem's work has become a mainstay of defense among charismatic groups and since calls for dialogue and unity between cessationists and noncessationists are being voiced based on his writings, his central thesis and major supporting arguments must be analyzed in order to determine their validity.

Delineation of Grudem's Hypothesis

Grudem offers his own definition of Christian prophecy, one that differs from traditional understanding. He writes, "Prophecy in ordinary New Testament churches was not equal to Scripture in authority but was simply a very human - and sometimes partially mistaken - report of something the Holy Spirit brought to someone's mind." New Testament prophecy consists of "telling something God has spontaneously brought to mind." In another place, he terms New Testament prophecy as "an unreliable human speech act in response to a revelation from the Holy Spirit." He admits that his concept is a "somewhat new definition of the nature of Christian prophecy."

He takes his definition from both cessationists and charismatics. In common with the former, he understands prophecy as non-competitive with the authority of the canonical New Testament because of the close of the canon at the end of the apostolic era. On the other hand, he concurs with the charismatic understanding that prophecy preserves "the spontaneous, powerful working of the Holy Spirit, giving 'edification, encouragement, and comfort,' which speaks directly to the needs of the moment and causes people to realize that 'truly God is among you.'" According to Grudem, Old Testament prophets are not comparable to New Testament prophets; instead, Old Testament prophets are to be compared with the New Testament apostles.

Consequently, New Testament prophets were "simply reporting in their own words what God would bring to mind, and . . . these prophecies did not have the authority of the words of the Lord."

> Much more commonly, prophet and prophecy were used of ordinary Christians who spoke not with absolute divine authority, but simply to report something God had laid on their hearts or brought to their minds. There are many indications in the New Testament that this ordinary gift of prophecy had authority less than that of the Bible, and even less than that of recognized Bible teaching in the early church.

In other words, prophecy depended on revelation from the Holy Spirit, but the prophet could understand it imperfectly, report it inaccurately, or both.

According to Grudem, only New Testament apostles spoke inspired words. Moreover, the words of the New Testament prophets were not inspired as were those of Old Testament prophets. This leaves him with two forms of New Testament prophecy: nonauthoritative "congregational" prophecy and authoritative (i.e., apostolic) prophecy.

The crucial point in Grudem's thesis is that the apostles, not the New Testament prophets, were the true successors of the Old Testament prophets and, like their earlier counterparts, spoke under the authority derived from the plenary verbal inspiration of their words. This apostolic gift is distinguished from the gift of prophecy exercised at Corinth (cf. 1 Cor. 12-14), Thessalonica (1 Thess. 5:19-21), Tyre (Acts 21:4), Ephesus (19:6), and by others such as Agabus (11:28; 21:10-11). Only the general content of this secondary prophecy can be vouched for, with allowances made for its being partially mistaken.

As a result, the New Testament gift of prophecy was allegedly open to being disobeyed without blame (Acts 21:4), being critically assessed by the whole congregation (1 Cor. 14:29) and being rejected outright as subordinate to Paul's apostolic revelations (vv. 37-38). According to Grudem, "these prophecies did not have the authority of the words of the Lord." Therefore, Grudem posits a sharp discontinuity between Old Testament prophets and New Testament prophets. New Testament prophets did not stand in line with their Old Testament counterparts. According to Grudem qualitative differences exist between Old Testament and New Testament prophets and prophecy, especially in their accuracy and authority.

Some Weaknesses of Grudem's Hypothesis

This newly proposed theory has multiple weaknesses. These show that Grudem's view contrasts with that of the New Testament concerning prophecy.

Continuity Of Old Testament And New Testament Prophecy

One of Grudem's fundamental assumptions is the positing of a sharp discontinuity between Old and New

Testament prophets. His case for an unauthoritative "congregational" prophecy in 1 Corinthians 12-14 and elsewhere in the New Testament rests on assuming a discontinuity between Old and New Testament prophecy. This premise of a strong discontinuity is fallacious for several reasons. Though these have been delineated in the two previous articles in this series, they are now applied directly to Grudem's hypothesis.

Standards for evaluating prophets in the post-apostolic church of the second century. The post-apostolic early church judged New Testament prophets on the basis of the standards set forth for prophets in the Old Testament. New Testament prophets who prophesied falsely were considered false prophets on the basis of Old Testament standards of evaluation. Thus, Grudem's assertion that New Testament prophets could be mistaken is not valid. Prophets in both eras who were wrong or inaccurate were shown to be false prophets by their false prophesying. As shown in the first article of this series, early post-apostolic Christians utilized Old Testament standards to judge later prophets. This may be seen, for example, by Anonymous's or Epiphanius's handling of the Montanist controversy. The criteria set forth in the Old Testament for prophets was used to condemn the excesses of Montanus and his followers for their false or "mistaken" prophecies.

Grudem also acknowledges that the Didache contains statements contradictory to his hypothesis. Didache 11 is directly contrary to his view that the authority of New Testament "congregational" prophecy does not extend to the words spoken by the prophets. Grudem admits that according to Didache 11.7, post-apostolic church prophets "were speaking with a divine authority that extended to their actual words." In 11.7, the Didache notes that "you must neither make trial of nor pass judgment on any prophet who speaks forth in the spirit. For every (other) sin will be forgiven, but this sin will not be forgiven" (cf.

Matt. 12:31). Here the thrust of the passage emphasizes that the authority of the New Testament prophet extended to the words of the prophecy uttered.

Grudem tries to counter this manifest contradiction to his hypothesis by stating that Didache 11.7 "almost directly contradicts Paul's instructions in 1 Corinthians 14:29" regarding the evaluation of prophets. Because of this, he hastily dismisses the data on New Testament prophets and prophecy supplied by the Didache in this verse and throughout the entire work. However, Grudem has erroneously interpreted 11.7. The way in which the Didache refers to a prophet as one "who speaks forth in the Spirit" (lalounta en pneumati, 11.7) indicates that a prophet was not to be tested while he was giving the prophecy. After setting forth the prophecy, a prophet's behavior and accuracy (i.e., the prophetic content) could be used as legitimate means of testing and determining the genuineness of the prophet (cf. Didache 11.8-12). Furthermore, according to Didache 11.11, while prophets may not be judged during their act of prophesying, their genuineness was to be judged by the community. In continuity with Paul's insistence that prophets and their prophecy be tested (1 Cor. 14:29) and John's instruction to test a prophet and his prophecy (1 John 4:1-3), the Didache asserts that prophets and their prophecies were to be tested. Though a surface reading of the Didache may give the impression that it rejects the testing of a prophet, an examination of the context of 11.8-12 makes it clear that this was not the case. The issue in testing seems to be the time of the testing rather than if a prophet was to be tested. Means of evaluating a true prophet are given in 11.8: "Not everyone who speaks forth in the Spirit is a prophet, but only if he has the kind of behavior which the Lord approves. From his behavior, then, will the false prophet and the true prophet be known." Prophets were to be judged on the basis of lack of greed for gain, consistency in doctrine and practice, and demonstration of knowing the ways of God. Therefore, this verse does not contradict 1 Corinthians 14:29 but stands in direct contradiction to Grudem's view. The Didache cannot be so easily dismissed.

An additional approach of Grudem is to dismiss the Didache completely as written by someone "who was out of touch with mainstream apostolic activity and teaching." Dismissing this evidence is convenient for his hypothesis. However, several arguments reveal his conclusion to be hasty. Although Eusebius places the Didache among the noncanonical books, some in the early church, such as Clement of Alexandria, appears to have understood it as Scripture. Athanasius said that while the work was not in the canon, it enjoyed a prominent position among books "appointed by the Fathers to be read by those who newly join us." Therefore, although the book admittedly is noncanonical, these citations indicate that it enjoyed high regard in the early church.

Some patristic scholars have argued for an early date for the Didache. Audet dates it around A.D. 60. Even if one does not agree with him, the Didache still reflects an early date. After an extensive discussion, Kraft concludes that the Didache evidences a great deal of Hellenistic Jewish material from early (i.e., first-century and early second-century) forms of Christianity. In light of this, beyond the fact that the Didache is not canonical, there is no substantial reason for rejecting its testimony in such a wholesale fashion as Grudem does. If the Didache is allowed to speak for itself, it stands in contradiction to his hypothesis. Contrary to Grudem's assertions, the Didache provides an important and early indication of how the post-apostolic early church regarded New Testament prophets and prophecy. The Didache substantiates the fact that New Testament prophets were considered fully authoritative in their prophetic pronouncements, even to the very words of the prophecy.

A final example must suffice with reference to the post-apostolic church fathers. Grudem cites Ignatius's Epistle to the Philadelphians 7.1-2. In 7.1 Ignatius wrote, "I cried out while I was with you, I spoke with a great voice, - with God's own voice, 'Give heed to the bishop, and to the presbytery and deacons.'" In 7.2, "the Spirit was preaching, and saying this, 'Do nothing without the bishop, keep your flesh as the temple of God, love unity, flee from divisions, be imitators of Jesus Christ, as was he also of his Father.'" Grudem presents this as an example supporting his contention for New Testament "congregational" prophecy having a content of a general kind (versus "apostolic" prophecy which extended to the very words): "The Holy Spirit was saying 'approximately this' or 'something like this.'"

Several arguments militate against Grudem's contention that Ignatius's prophecy supports Grudem's hypothesis. First, Ignatius claimed that he spoke with God's voice. This assertion would hardly support Grudem's contention that New Testament prophets could be mistaken, especially when Ignatius equated his prophecy with "God's own voice." This clearly intimates that New Testament "congregational" prophecy was considered totally authoritative in the post-apostolic early church. Second, Ignatius claimed to have supernatural knowledge of the divisions in the Philadelphian community of believers. This information did not come "from any human being" but from the Holy Spirit (7.2). He rested the accuracy and authority of his prophecies on the miraculous source of his information. For Ignatius, the Holy Spirit served as the guarantor of the accuracy of his prophesying. Third, Grudem's assertion that the prophecy of 7.2 is a "summary" of 7.1, which supports his contention for prophecy of "general content," is doubtful. The prophecy of 7.2 supplies too much precise information for Grudem's argument to be valid that 7.2 summarizes 7.1. Ignatius seems to have given a separate prophecy in 7.2, which added additional explicit prophetic content to that of 7.1. Fourth, Ignatius introduced his prophecy in 7.2 by the phrase to pneuma ... legon tade, the same phrase used in both the Old and New Testaments to introduce exact ("word-for-word") prophetic content (Ezek. 6:1; 7:2; 11:17; Amos 1:3, 9, 13; 2:4; Acts 21:10-11; Rev. 2:1, 8, 12, 18; 3:1, 7, 14, etc.). This phrase signals a conscious attempt by Ignatius to imitate biblical prophets who were considered inspired in the very words they utilized in prophecy. In light of this, it is more likely that Ignatius considered his prophecy to be "word-for-word" inspired and fully authoritative rather than only "generally" inspired in content.

In summary, when the data from the post-apostolic church fathers are viewed closely, support for Grudem's contention melts away. Instead, the data support the contention for fully authoritative and accurate prophecy as maintained by the central thrusts of this series.

New Testament prophecy founded on Old Testament prophecy. The discussion of the quotation of Joel 2:28-32 in Acts 2:17-21 has shown that New Testament prophecy is founded on and has a significant continuity with Old Testament prophetic phenomenon and experience. Indeed, Peter linked this beginning of New Testament prophecy with the prophetic phenomena of the Old Testament. The verse establishes a fundamental continuity between the Old and New Testament prophecy. This fundamental continuity contradicts Grudem's hypothesis that posits a substantial difference between Old Testament and New Testament prophets and prophecy.

Similarity of vocabulary and phraseology for Old Testament and New Testament prophets. It has been shown that the New Testament vocabulary and phraseology referring to both prophets and prophecy serve as a strong indication that the New Testament did not conceptualize any significant differences in prophetic expression between Old and New Testament prophets. Since the vocabulary and phraseology are the same, this would also indicate that the New Testament authors conceived of the existence of a fundamental continuity between these two eras of prophecy.

Importantly, the New Testament vocabulary is also uniform in referring to various New Testament prophets. Grudem's proposed identification of two forms of prophecy rests on differentiating prophecy in 1 Corinthians 12-14 from prophecy in Ephesians 2:20 and 3:5, the latter being "apostolic" prophecy and the former being "congregational" prophecy. An inherent weakness in this distinction is reflected in a close scrutiny of technical terms used in both sections. The same "clusters" of revelational-type words occur in 1 Corinthians 12-14 as occur in the context of Ephesians 2-3. For example, profhthj and profteuw are used in both (1 Cor. 12:28; 13:9; 14:1-6, 24, 31-32, 37, 39; Eph. 2:20; 3:5). So are oikodomh and oikodomew (1 Cor. 14:3-5, 12, 17, 26; Eph. 2:20-21), musthrion (1 Cor. 13:2; 14:2; Eph. 3:3-4, 9), apokalupsij and apokaluptw (1 Cor. 14:6, 26, 30; Eph. 3:3, 5), kruptw and its cognates (1 Cor. 14:25; Eph. 3:9), apostoloj (1 Cor. 12:28-29; Eph. 2:20; 3:5), and sofia (1 Cor. 12:8; Eph. 3:10). Grouping such technical terminology in a single context signals a reference to direct divine communication to an authoritative prophet. The presence of this type of communication in Ephesians 2-3 is not in doubt, and no significant basis exists for questioning a reference to it in 1 Corinthians 12-14. So the case for contrasting "congregational" prophecy with "apostolic" prophecy falters at another point.

In light of the evidence, Grudem's premise of a sharp discontinuity between Old and New Testament prophecy is doubtful.

Grammatically Related Weaknesses

Misuse of Sharp's rule. In the second article in this series, it was shown that Ephesians 2:20 indicates that apostles and New Testament prophets constituted the foundation of the church. As such, both apostles and New Testament prophets were involved in the important reception of revelation regarding such doctrines as Gentile inclusion in the composition of the church (Eph. 3:5-9). In contrast to this, Grudem interprets Ephesians 2:20 to mean "the apostles who are also prophets" solely constituted the doctrinal foundation of the church, thereby excluding New Testament prophets from such a foundational role. Grudem's most significant argument for equating "apostles" with "prophets" in Ephesians 2:20 stems from an application of a grammatical rule dealing with two nouns connected by the Greek word "kai" ("and") and governed by only one article. His argument is seriously flawed.

Regarding Ephesians 2:20 he writes,

> The absence of the second article in "touj de poimenaj kai didaskalouj" that the writer views the apostles and prophets as a single group, and that we cannot immediately be sure whether that group has one or two components. But the grammatical structure clearly allows for the possibility that one group with one component is meant, for there are several instances in the New Testament where one definite article governs two or more nouns joined by "kai" and it is clear that one group with only one component (or one person) is implied. In Ephesians 4:11 it is noteworthy: "edwken touj men apostolouj, touj de profhtaj, touj de euaggelistaj, touj de poimenaj kai didaskalouj". The pastors and teachers are the same people but two different functions are named.

At this point Grudem lists "most of the clear examples of this type of construction from the Pauline corpus, along with some scattered examples from elsewhere in the New Testament." His list includes examples of the same person described with two or more titles (Rom. 16:7; Eph. 4:11; 6:21; Phil. 2:25; Col. 1:2; 4:7; Phile. 1; Heb. 3:l; I Pet. 2:25; 2 Pet. 3:18), phrases in which God is named with a similar form (Rom. 15:6; 2 Cor. 1:3; 11:31; Gal. 1:4; Eph. 1:3; 5:20; Phil. 4:20; Col. 1:3; 3:17; 1 Thess. 1:3; 3:11 [twice]; 1 Tim. 6:15; Titus 2:13; 2 Pet. 1:1, 11), nonpersonal objects occasionally referred to in this way (1 Thess. 3:7; Titus 2:13), and participles and infinitives in this type of construction (1 Cor. 11:29; Gal. 1:7; 1 Thess. 5:12). Grudem concludes,

> This does not imply that Eph. 2:20 must mean "the apostles who are also prophets," for there are many other examples which could be listed where one group with two distinct components is named (cf. Acts 13:50). Nevertheless, it must be noted that I was unable to find in the Pauline corpus even one clear example analogous to Acts 13:50 or 15:2, where two distinct people or classes of people (as opposed to things) are joined by kai and only one article is used. This may be more or less significant, depending in part on one's view of the authorship of Ephesians. But it should not be overlooked that when Paul wants to distinguish two people or groups he does not hesitate to use a second article (1 Cor. 3:8; 8:6; etc.; cf. Eph. 3:10). And I have listed above over twenty Pauline examples where clearly one person or group is implied by this type of construction.

So Eph. 2:20 views "the apostles and prophets" as one group. Grammatically, that group could have two components, but such an interpretation would not be exactly in accord with Pauline usage. If the author had meant to speak of a two-component group he certainly did not make this meaning very clear to his readers (as he could have done by adding another twn before profhtwn). On the other hand, the large number of New Testament parallels shows that "the apostles who are also prophets" would have easily been understood by the readers if other factors in the context allowed for or favored this interpretation.

From this, he concludes that Ephesians 2:20 is speaking of apostle-prophets who are distinguished from those who are simply prophets described in other passages such as 1 Corinthians 12-14. apostle-prophets, he says, were limited to the first-century church, but the other kind continues to the present day.

Though the case for this interpretation of Ephesians 2:20 may appear impressive, it is problematic for a number of reasons. Basically, it rests on a fundamental error and a commonly misunderstood application of Sharp's rule. The rule is as follows:

> When the copulative kai connects nouns of the same case [viz. nouns (either substantive or adjective, or participles) of personal description, respecting office, dignity, affinity, or connection, and attributes, properties, or qualities, good or ill] if the article o, or any of its cases, precedes the first of the said nouns or participles, and is not repeated before the second noun or participle, the latter always relates to the same person that is expressed or described by the first noun or participle: i.e., it denotes a further description of the first named person.

Though challenged repeatedly, no one has succeeded in overturning or refuting it insofar as the New Testament is concerned.

Yet four lesser known stipulations of Sharp's rule are often overlooked. These must be met if the two nouns in the construction are to be viewed as referring to the same person. They are these: (a) both nouns must be personal; (b) both nouns must be common nouns, that is, not proper names; (c) both nouns must be in the same case, and (d) both nouns must be singular. Sharp did not clearly delineate these stipulations in conjunction with his first rule, so most grammars are ambiguous in these areas.

Many exegetes, including Grudem, reflect no awareness of these qualifications and hence apply Sharp's rule without proper refinements. For instance, though the fourth stipulation about the rule's limitation to singular nouns only was not clearly stated in the first rule, a perusal of Sharp's monograph reveals that he insisted that the rule applies absolutely to the singular only. The limitation may be inferred by an argument from silence in his statement of the rule: "the latter always relates to the same person . . . i.e., it denotes a further description of the first-named person." Later in the monograph he offers this clarification: "There is no exception or instance of the like mode of expression that I know of, which necessarily requires [that] a construction be different from what is laid down, except that the nouns be proper names, or in the plural number, in which there are numerous exceptions." Again at another point, he states that impersonal constructions are within the purview of the second, third, fifth, and sixth rules, but not the first or fourth.

Middleton, whose early study on the Greek article is still highly respected, was the first Greek grammarian to accept the validity of Sharp's rule. He notes many exceptions to Sharp's rule when plural nouns are involved.

> What reason can be alleged, why the practice in Plural Attributives should differ from that in Singular ones? The circumstances are evidently dissimilar. A single individual may

stand in various relations and act in divers capacities. . . . But this does not happen in the same degree with respect to Plurals. Though one individual may act, and frequently does act, in several capacities, it is not likely that a multitude of individuals should all of them act in the same several capacities.

On the basis of an extensive analysis of plural nouns in comparable constructions in the New Testament, Wallace affirms that plural nouns are an exception to Sharp's rule. He has cited many passages where the members of the construction cannot be equated with each other and they thus constitute clear exceptions (e.g., Matt. 3:7; 17:1; 27:56; Acts 17:12). His conclusion is, "Granville Sharp applied his rule only to singular, non-proper, personal nouns of the same case." Wallace has cataloged the abuse of Sharp's rule by several grammatical works considered standards in the field of New Testament grammar. Regarding this abuse he notes,

"But what about the abuse of the rule? Almost without exception, those who seem to be acquainted with Sharp's rule and agree with its validity misunderstand and abuse it. Virtually no one is exempt from this charge-grammarians, commentators, theologians alike are guilty. Typically, the rule is usually perceived to extend to plural and impersonal constructions-in spite of the fact that the evidence of the New Testament with reference to plural and impersonal nouns is contrary to this supposition.

Moreover, he cites several well-known grammarians to illustrate his point.

Although most commentaries consider the two terms ["pastors" and "teachers"] to refer to one group, we must emphatically insist that such a view has no grammatical basis, even though

> the writers who maintain this view almost unanimously rest their case on the supposed semantics of the article-noun-kai-construction. Yet, as we have seen, there are no other examples in the New Testament of this construction with nouns in the plural, either clearly tagged or ambiguous, which allow for such a possibility. One would, therefore, be on rather shaky ground to insist on such a nuance here [Eph. 4:11]-especially if the main weapon in his arsenal is syntax!

Wallace affirms the validity of the rule for plural adjectives or participles but indicates he has found no clear instances of the rule's applicability to plural nouns in the New Testament Koine Greek, papyri, or Hellenistic or classical Greek.

This refined application of Sharp's rule removes Grudem's major foundation for equating apostles and prophets, since the rule is not applicable to Ephesians 2:20. In this verse Paul designated two separate groups, apostles and New Testament prophets, without equating one to the other. Since the passage labels prophecy as a foundational gift, the conclusion is that New Testament prophecy has ceased along with the gift of apostleship.

Invalid cross-references. Furthermore, the cross-references Grudem cites to support an equation of apostles and prophets are invalid, because each of the examples is semantically unparallel. Not one is a clear example of an application of Sharp's rule to plural nouns, as Grudem's position on Ephesians 2:20 requires. Many of the cross-references are singular nouns governed by a single article, to which Sharp's rule does apply, so long as the nouns are personal and not proper nouns. These are a different grammatical entity from the plural-noun construction in Ephesians 2:20 and do not support his view of this verse. Sharp's rule is applicable to a few plural adjectives (e.g.,

Rom. 16:7; Col. 1:2), but the same principle does not apply to plural-noun constructions. This difference also holds between plural participles (e.g., Gal. 1:7; 1 Thess. 5:12) and plural nouns. Grudem's use of impersonal nouns as a grammatical parallel is also inaccurate (e.g., 1 Thess. 3:7) because Sharp's rule requires personal nouns. Space forbids an exhaustive citation of all the alleged parallels, but each of them is nonparallel for one of these reasons.

Thus none of the cross-references cited supports identification of prophets with apostles in Ephesians 2:20, since none of Grudem's cross-references presents an analogous construction. It is wrong, therefore, for him to base his view on this verse.

Disregard for Ephesians 4:11. Another weakness in Grudem's reasoning regarding the equation of apostles and prophets in Ephesians 2:20 lies in his use of Ephesians 4:11 for support. Two aspects of Ephesians 4:11 militate against his conclusion. First, he argues, "When Paul wants to distinguish two people or groups he does not hesitate to use a second article." On this basis, he concludes that the single article with apostle and prophets in 2:20 dictates that Paul intended to equate the two. Yet in Ephesians 4:11-a verse that he uses in another way as a supporting grammatical analogy - Paul used two articles, one with "apostles" and one with "prophets": ("edwken touj men apostolouj, touj de profhtaj", "on one hand he gave apostles and on the other, prophets") which clearly delineates New Testament prophets as a group separate from the apostles. It is cogent reasoning that since Paul thus distinguishes between apostles and prophets in 4:11, he must have intended the same distinction in 2:20. This belies Grudem's interpretation. Second, as already noted, the grammatical analogy that Grudem cites in Ephesians 4:11-that is, the identification of "pastors" and "teachers"- provides no support for his theory, because the plural nouns forbid the pressing of Sharp's rule here too.

Prestige Of New Testament Prophets

Another weakness in Grudem's hypothesis is his failure to recognize the high degree of prestige enjoyed by New Testament prophets in the Christian community. As already shown from a correct understanding of Ephesians 2:20, New Testament prophets, in association with the apostles, held the honorable status of helping lay the foundation of the church. Their ranking in the list of gifted persons in 1 Corinthians 12:28 (cf. 14:1) places them second only to the apostles in usefulness to the body of Christ. As Geisler notes, "This exalted position Paul gives to the gift of prophecy is further indication that it [New Testament prophecy] is neither fallible nor inferior to the gift of prophecy in the Old Testament."

New Testament prophets, along with the apostles, were recipients of special revelation regarding the mystery of the inclusion of Jews and Gentiles in the one universal body of Christ. The presence of Gentiles in such a relationship was unrevealed before the New Testament era (Eph 3:5) but came to apostles and New Testament prophets as inspired utterances and writings such as the canonical Book of Ephesians. Reception and propagation of such revelation constituted the foundation of the church universal throughout the present age. New Testament prophets were vehicles for these revelations and held a high profile among early Christians for this reason.

In light of this, Grudem's words do not match the high status of prophets upheld in the New Testament: "Prophecy in ordinary New Testament churches was not equal to Scripture in authority but was simply a very human-and sometimes partially mistaken-report of something that the Holy Spirit brought to someone's mind." Such a relegation of prophecy to a lesser status raises the question of how the early church could have guarded itself against hopeless doctrinal confusion. If prophets were at times used to convey inspired revelations and at other times were nonauthoritative and mistaken, who could distinguish their authoritative and accurate messages from the other kind?

The Need for Constant Evaluation of New Testament Prophecy

Grudem uses the call for evaluation of prophetic utterances in 1 Corinthians 14:29-31 as an argument for the existence of nonauthoritative congregational prophecy. He maintains that Old Testament prophets were never challenged in this way because of the high regard in which they were held. For him, this signals a great difference between Old Testament and New Testament prophets; that is, New Testament prophets were not so prestigious. After an Old Testament prophet was evaluated and accepted as a true prophet of God, his words were never questioned, but each prophecy of a New Testament prophet, Grudem argues, had to be evaluated. Herein lies a contrast, causing Grudem to conclude that the New Testament gift operated at a lower level of authority.

However, several arguments render Grudem's hypothesis tenuous. First, the needed critical evaluation resulted from a changed status of believers under the New Covenant. In accord with Joel 2:28-32 and Acts 2:17-21, the Holy Spirit was poured out on all believers. This does not mean that all Christians would be prophets, a possibility Paul negated in 1 Corinthians 12:29, "all are not prophets, are they?" It did, however, create the potential, according to Joel and Acts, that the gift of prophecy would be much more widely disseminated than to a limited group of prophets like those who spoke for the Lord in the theocratic community under the Old Covenant. As noted in the second article of this series, this expanded sphere of prophetic activity increased the need for care in discerning true prophecies from false prophecies.

This is the need Paul tried to meet in 1 Corinthians 14:29-31. The larger the group of prophets, the more potential there was for abuse of prophecy by those who were not New Testament prophets. This danger became a reality in the latter part of the first century and beyond, as evidenced by John's warning: "Beloved, do not believe every spirit, but test the spirits to see whether they are from God; because many false prophets have gone out into the world" (1 John 4:1; cf. 2 Pet. 2:1-22; Jude 4, 11-16).

Second, Grudem's picture of Old Testament prophecy and its prestige is highly idealized and rather unrealistic. His idealized picture is obtained substantially from historical hindsight rather than from an examination of the actual state of affairs existing at the time of the Old Testament prophets. A brief review reveals four relevant features of Old Testament prophecy: (1) The Israelites frequently disobeyed Old Testament prophets (such as Samuel, Elisha, and Jeremiah, to name only a few), even when their proclamations were authoritative as the very words of the Lord (e.g., 1 Sam. 13:8-14; Jer. 36:1-32), and put the prophets to flight, threatening to kill them (e.g., 1 Kings 19:1-3). Amos's preaching in Bethel aroused such opposition that he had to flee from Bethel for his life (Amos 7:10-17). (2) Some prophets enjoyed greater status and prestige than others who were less famous (e.g., an unknown prophet in 1 Kings 20:35-43; cf. also 19:10). (3) The people threatened and otherwise strongly opposed some prophets like Jeremiah because of their status as prophets of the Lord. Jeremiah could hardly have been said to have enjoyed much of an authoritative status in Israel at such times, because his hearers disobeyed him, despised him, rejected him, beat him, and imprisoned him because of his prophetic ministry (e.g., Jer. 11:18-23; 12:6; 18:18; 20:1-3; 26:1-24; 37:11-38:28). (4) According to Jewish tradition, some prophets like Isaiah were tortured and assassinated rather than given great honor (cf. 1 Kings 18:13).

Third, Jesus' words in Matthew 23:37 that Israel consistently despised, rejected, and killed her prophets hardly conveys the impression of great respect afforded the Old Testament prophets by their contemporaries. Nor does it suggest that their message was never questioned or rejected (cf. Heb. 11:33-40).

Old Testament prophets became revered only by later generations of Jewish people. They had little such prominence during their lifetime. Only as later generations reflected on their idolatrous past and disobedience to the prophets did the prophets gain a place of great esteem in the eyes of the people (cf. Ezra 9:1-11). This elite group of Old Testament spokesmen for the Lord experienced the anointing and influence of the Holy Spirit in a way that was not appreciated by their immediate listeners.

Fourth, the New Testament standard for evaluating prophets is comparable to relevant guidelines in the Old Testament. Deuteronomy 13 and 18 set forth the policy that a prophet was to be judged by his prophesyings. Prophets were considered to be false on the basis of false prophesying. In the second century A.D., these same Old Testament principles and guidelines were used by Epiphanius and Anonymous to refute the Montanist heresy. Therefore, these Old Testament standards for evaluating prophecies were applied to prophets as a basis for judging true from false prophets before, during, and after the New Testament era. As Saucy notes regarding the Pauline stipulation to evaluate prophecies, "This principle does not appear to be different than in the Old Testament and therefore does not seem persuasive of two levels of prophetic activity." The New Testament furnishes no indication that New Testament-era Jews, particularly those who became apostles in the early church, considered the requirements for prophets in the Old Testament to have been abrogated or essentially modified in the New Testament.

Identification of Evaluators

Another weakness in Grudem's theory regarding New Testament prophecy is his method of handling 1 Corinthians 14:29, which reads, "And let two or three prophets speak, and let the others pass judgment." A critical issue in this statement concerns the identity of those "passing judgment" or "discerning" the validity of alleged prophetic pronouncements. Grudem raises a psychological point.

> If we understand oi alloi to be restricted to a special group of prophets, we have much difficulty picturing what the rest of the congregation would do during the prophecy and judging. Would they sit during the prophecy waiting for the prophecy to end and be judged before knowing whether to believe any part of it? . . . Especially hard to believe is the idea that the teachers, administrators and other church leaders without special gifts of prophecy would sit passively awaiting the verdict of an elite group.

Aside from the fact that this argumentation is nonexegetical in nature, it is weak in that reason and logic, to which he appeals, can also dictate that not everyone in the congregation would be in a position to evaluate prophecy, especially in a public setting. Admittedly 1 John 4:1-3 urges a testing of spirits in a general sense by all Christians because of false prophecy and teaching, but Paul clearly indicated in 1 Corinthians 12:10 (regarding the "distinguishing of spirits") that not everyone possessed that special ability. That gift was dispensed to a limited number according to the sovereign will of the Holy Spirit (1 Cor. 12:11; cf. v. 18). It is conspicuous that those possessing special ability in discerning were better equipped to pass judgment on congregational prophecies than the ones who did not possess the gift. This differentiation in evaluative capabilities within the congregation raises a loud contextual objection to the view that all members of the congregation in 1 Corinthians 14:29 were supposed to evaluate the prophets.

The most natural and grammatical antecedent of oi alloi in 14:29 is profhtai in the first half of the verse. Paul's use of alloj rather than eteroj indicates his intention to designate the same category of persons as those just referred to. Referring "the others" to other prophets is further confirmed by the use of allwj immediately afterward in verse 30, where it is an evident reference to "another" prophet. This repetition of the same adjective, "other" or "another," shows that Paul still had prophets in mind when he used oi alloi in verse 29. In this statement, then, where interpretation is tedious, the contextual probabilities rest on the side of identifying those who evaluate prophetic utterances of others as being the prophets who apparently possessed the gift of discerning of spirits along with their prophetic gift.

Those prophets were to pass judgment on what other prophets said to ascertain whether their utterances came from the Holy Spirit or not. Just as interpretation was needed in conjunction with the exercise of tongues (1 Cor. 12:10c), discernment was needed to accompany prophecy (v. 10b). Inspired spokesmen were in the best position to judge spontaneously whether a new utterance agreed with Paul's teaching (cf. Gal. 1:8-9; 2 Thess. 2:1-3) and generally accepted beliefs of the Christian community (1 Cor. 12:1-3).

As noted in the second article in this series, the context of 1 Corinthians 12:3 also sheds light on the need for evaluating prophets addressed in 14:29. Apparently, false prophets had preached that Jesus was accursed (12:3) even though they professed to be true prophets. In the face of such starkly erroneous prophesying, Paul warned them to evaluate each prophecy carefully to ensure that a genuine prophet had spoken. Some recognized voice was needed to declare whether the Holy Spirit was the source of that statement or that the person voicing a declaration was a false prophet.

Thus 1 Corinthians 14:29 does not necessarily mean that established prophets had to be verified continually. Yet this passage does set down the general principle that any potential prophet needed to be scrutinized by other prophets. This principle invalidates Grudem's conclusion that a genuine prophet's message contained a mixture of truth and error. The guideline established merely enforces the need for careful analysis of any prophet who claimed to speak by the Spirit of God to determine the source of his message. Once his source was identified as God, further examination was most likely unnecessary. The Holy Spirit served as the guarantor of the accuracy of the true prophet. Moreover, according to 2 Corinthians 11:13-15, even false prophets had potential to feign a true prophecy, so Paul encouraged a continued vigil. The regular ministry of prophets was to ensure the genuineness of prophets and prophecies as a safeguard against doctrinal heresies.

In summary, judging a prophecy does not imply that the gift could result in errant pronouncements. The responsibility of New Testament prophets to weigh the prophecies of others does not imply that true prophets were capable of giving false prophecies, but that false prophets could disguise their falsity by occasional true utterances.

The Interruption of Prophecies

Closely associated with the evaluation of prophecies is Grudem's contention that because a New Testament prophet's prophesying could be interrupted, the prophecy was nonauthoritative or fallible, that is, not from God (1 Cor. 14:30-32). According to Grudem, such an interruption would mean that the remainder of the prophecy could be lost. This interruption and supposed loss of the prophecy signals that the prophetic content was less authoritative; otherwise, Paul would have shown "more concern for the preservation of these words and their proclamation to the church."

However, because a prophecy could be interrupted does not in any way imply that the prophesying of the New Testament prophet was inferior or that some of the content of the prophecy could be lost. The thrust of verses 30-32 is that if a revelation is from God, the prophet will remain in conscious control of his mind and will. In other words, a prophecy which is truly from God is evidenced by an orderly and rational manner of presentation. Geisler stresses the need to consider the cultural and religious environment at Corinth in evaluating these verses.

The fact that prophets could be interrupted does not imply that their message was not from God. Rather, it reveals that "the spirits of prophets are subject to control of prophets" (1 Corinthians 14:32). Ecstatic utterances were common among pagans, such as the Corinthians once were. In these occult prophecies, the one giving the utterances was overpowered by the spirit giving the utterances. By contrast, Paul is saying that if a revelation is truly from God, then the prophet will remain in conscious control of his mind and will. In short, if it is really of God, it can wait.

The Shepherd of Hermas also reflects this same principle that the genuine prophet remains in rational control while supernatural power inspires him during the prophetic utterance. However, in dealing with the Montanists, Anonymous dismissed their prophesyings as irrationally ecstatic based on his understanding of Old Testament prophets who remained rational even in the prophetic state. Hence interruption of New Testament prophets does not imply some inferior form of "congregational" prophecy as maintained by Grudem. Orderly procedures (and possibility of interruption) functioned as a guard against irrationally ecstatic prophets (i.e., false prophets).

Apostolic Authority Versus New Testament Prophetic Pronouncements

Grudem also contends that in 1 Corinthians 14:37-38 Paul rated the authority of Christian prophets below his own authority. Grudem uses this to support his view that New Testament prophetic authority was inferior to that of the apostles and hence inferior to Old Testament prophets also. According to this view Paul's claim of authority in this passage means that New Testament "congregational" prophecy had less authority than "apostolic" prophecy. This understanding of Paul's words is not probable for important reasons. First, in 1 Corinthians 14:37-38 Paul was more likely asserting that if a Christian prophet is truly from God, his prophecies will concur with apostolic truth (cf. Gal. 1:8-9). False prophets and teachers constantly challenged apostolic authority and doctrine (e.g., Gal. 2:4-5; 2 Tim. 2:18; cf. Jude 3). In light of his own apostolic office, Paul's comparison between the Corinthian claims of authority and his own is best understood to teach that true prophets and their prophecies would be consistent with apostolic truth and would recognize Paul's words and commandments as coming directly from the Lord Jesus Christ. Any alleged prophet opposing apostolic standards and elevating himself to the role of God's only spokesman (1 Cor. 14:36) was to be recognized as false and his authority rejected (v. 38).

Second, apostolic authority must be distinguished from prophetic authority. Saucy's point is pertinent.

Rather than seeing the differences in the authority of prophecy, it seems that the solution lies in the personal authority of an apostle of Jesus Christ. Both Paul's prophecy and true prophecies in the church were words inspired by the Spirit of God. Paul, however, in distinction from prophets of the church, carried personal authority as the commissioned representative of Christ.

This personal authority as an apostle does not mean that Paul's prophecies were any more authoritative than those of an anonymous Christian prophet. When an apostle prophesied, and an anonymous Christian prophet utilized his or her gift, both were equally authoritative and infallible because the Source of both apostolic prophecy and Christian prophets was the Holy Spirit.

Conclusion

In light of the substantial negation of the major premises of Grudem's hypothesis, his assertions regarding two forms of New Testament prophecy cannot stand. Close examination of his hypothesis reveals critical weaknesses and also outright contradictions of the biblical data. Hence this major justification of the practice of "congregational" prophecy among such charismatic groups as the Vineyard and Sign and Wonders movements evaporates. The idea of a bifurcation of the prophetic gift into two distinct forms has no support either from the biblical data or from the church's handling of the Montanist controversy in the second century. Such a hypothesis is also invalid for promoting dialogue between cessationist and noncessationist camps, because it does not provide valid grounds for the justification of the present practice of prophecy among noncessationist groups. Grudem's hypothesis also should be viewed with alarm. Since prophecy has the assumption of revelational authority from the Holy Spirit, the idea of "mistaken" prophecy has the potential of doing untold harm to the church.

The fourth and final article in this series will deal with the question of the cessation of the prophetic gift. Various reasons will be delineated to demonstrate that miraculous gifts like New Testament prophecy are no longer in operation in the worship and practice of the church.

CHAPTER 4 "When Will the Gift of Prophecy Cease?"

In discussing the cessation of New Testament prophecy, two essential areas should be examined. First, prophecy's miraculous nature must be stressed. Because prophecy is a miraculous gift mediated by the Holy Spirit, any attempt at describing or defining the gift without proper consideration of this element may result in a marked misunderstanding of the nature and operation of prophecy. Current novel attempts at defining prophecy impugn the miraculous nature of New Testament prophecy. True New Testament prophets declared Spirit-inspired messages that were fully authoritative and completely accurate-not "merely human words" that could be "mistaken" or accepted and rejected by the congregation on a "take it or leave it" basis.

Second, strategic arguments demonstrate that the gift of prophecy, like the other miraculous gifts of apostleship and tongues, has ceased. The gift of prophecy played a vital role in the foundational aspects of the church. With the church firmly established through the ministry of the first-century apostles and New Testament prophets, prophecy passed from the scene.

The Miraculous Nature of New Testament Prophecy

In both the Old and New Testaments, prophecy's essential nature is that of a miraculous gift involving the direct reception of revelatory information from God to the prophet. This miraculous nature of prophecy can be demonstrated in several ways. The following facts illustrate the supernatural character of the prophetic gift.

The Prophet as Spokesperson for the Lord

The chief function of the prophet (profhvth") or of prophecy (profhteiva) was not necessarily found in the element of prediction of future events. Though prediction was an important factor in the prophetic role, the predictive aspect is considered a later development in the significance of the word group.

A primary function of the prophet in both extrabiblical and biblical usage was to proclaim or announce the will of God to the people. As such, the prophet was the "immediately inspired spokesman" for God. Since every prophet declared something that was not his own, the synonym that comes closest to the primary function of the prophet is the Greek word kh'rux (verb, khruvssw), for the kh'rux also declared what he had received from another. Thus the profhvth" occupies a mediatorial role, for he was both the mouthpiece of and spokesman for God. In that role a prophet had the potential to claim much authority in a believing community, particularly since he announced the will of God to His people.

This primary function of the biblical prophet as spokesman or mouthpiece for the Lord also underscores the essentially miraculous nature of both Old and New Testament prophecy.

That is, the basic nature of the genuine biblical prophet was someone who, through the inspired prophetic state, was in direct contact with God in the performance of his gift in a way that others were not. Prophecy's miraculous nature centers strategically in the supernatural reception of revelation from God to the prophet. Importantly, such a gift had to be completely miraculous in character, for if that gift did not involve a Spirit-mediated, miraculous element, the community could not guard itself against doctrinal confusion and error.

Prophecy and Revelation

As noted in the second article in this series, prophecy is a sovereignly bestowed charisma through which revelations from God occur (1 Cor. 2:10; 12:10; 13:9; 14:6, 29). The same gift of prophecy was active whether the revelation involved canonical matters or the impartation of immediate guidance to the church (e.g., the writing of the Book of Revelation [Rev. 1:10] or the command of the Holy Spirit through church prophets to send out Barnabas and Saul [Acts 13:1-4]). Also, the same gift was involved whether that revelation came from apostles who possessed the gift of prophecy or from nonapostolic New Testament prophets (Eph. 2:20; 3:5; 1 Cor. 14:29-31). For this reason, prophecy involved speech based on direct reception of revelatory information from God through the prophet(s) which, in turn, guided the people of God in matters of faith and practice.

Furthermore, the revelation did not have to entail exclusively predictive elements to be miraculous. Such a statement does not minimize the predictive characteristic exhibited in prophecy, for prophecy is frequently predictive, but it reduces prophecy to its primary characteristic of Spirit-inspired speech based on direct revelatory communication from God involving information which often could not be known on an ordinary, human basis. Even prediction involves the communication of divine truth which could not be known by ordinary means, that is, supernatural communication between God and the prophet.

The inclusion of Gentiles in the church (Eph. 3:5-10) illustrates this point. This concept revealed through the apostles and New Testament prophets to the church, is primarily doctrinal and does not necessarily encompass prediction. The revelatory nature of Paul's message did not involve solely predictive elements but also reception of the true nature of the gospel of Jesus Christ and justification by faith (Acts 9:3-6, 20; Gal. 1:12, 16-17). In Acts 13:1-3, God revealed His will through the prophets regarding sending Barnabas and Saul on their first Gentile mission. In Matthew 26:67-68 (cf. Mark 14:65 and Luke 22:64), the Jews sarcastically asked Jesus to prophesy who hit Him, thus indicating supernatural discernment but not necessarily requiring prediction. In John 4:19 the woman at the well perceived Jesus to be a prophet, not on the basis of prediction, but because of His miraculous knowledge of her marital history. Luke 7:39 indicates that the Pharisees considered a prophet to have supernatural discernment of the true character of people. In 1 Corinthians 14:29-31 prophets are linked with the miraculous ability to determine true prophets from false prophets rather than merely setting forth predictive prophecies (cf. 12:10). Hence the miraculous nature of prophecy has its basis in the reception of revelation. Such revelation frequently involved the reception of information that exceeded normal human cognitive functions. As spokespersons for God, biblical prophets in both Testaments distinguished themselves as prophets primarily by the possession of a supernatural ability to receive revelations directly from God. Therefore prophecy, reduced to its basic function, is Spirit-inspired utterance based on the direct, miraculous reception of divine revelation.

Another important point about the miraculous nature of prophecy must be addressed, namely, wrongly equating prophecy with mere comfort, admonishment, or encouragement. This reflects a fundamental misunderstanding of 1 Corinthians 14:3 in which Paul says that "one who prophesies speaks to men for edification and exhortation and consolation." However, Paul was not defining prophesy but, in context, "merely uses the fact that prophecy is understandable and therefore results in edification, exhortation, and encouragement." Since prophecy, in contrast to tongues, contributed directly to the understanding of the congregation, it had an edifying effect on the whole group, including the speaker (1 Cor. 14:4). Godet notes,

> The conclusion is often drawn from this verse, that since to prophesy is to edify, exhort, comfort, whoever edifies, exhorts, comforts, merits according to Paul the title prophet. This reasoning is as just as it would be to say: He who runs moves his legs; therefore, whoever moves his legs, runs; or, to take a more nearly related example: He who speaks to God in a tongue, speaks to God; and therefore whoever speaks to God, is a glossalalete. No, certainly; one may edify, comfort, encourage, without deserving the title of prophet or prophetess.

These latter concepts are better viewed as the results of prophecy and not as references to the content of prophecy. Hence the result of prophecy was edification, exhortation, and comfort.

For example, the Book of Revelation is labeled "revelation" (ajpokavluyi") and also as "prophecy" (profhteiva") that John the prophet received in the prophetic state (ejgenovmhn ejn pneuvmati, Rev. 1:10) directly from Jesus Christ or angelic ministers (1:1). Brown notes, "Although the words parakaleand paraklsis do not occur, the letters to the seven churches (chs. 2 and 3) and indeed the whole work constitutes a series of messages of consolation and exhortation. The work carries the authority of the exalted Christ, speaking through the Spirit (Rev. 22:18 f.)." The vast portion of the Book of Revelation exhibits the miraculous element of predictive prophecy in which John was transported to the future (chaps. 4-22). Even in the messages to the seven churches, which are considered "historical" in nature (i.e., chaps. 2-3 written to seven historical churches-"the things which are" [cf. 1:19]), miraculous elements predominate. For instance supernatural knowledge of the spiritual conditions of these churches emphasizes the miraculous nature of these messages (e.g., Rev. 2:2-6, 9-10, 19-28; 3:2, 4-5, 7-12, 15-18), which brought comfort to some churches (e.g., Smyrna, 2:8-11, and Philadelphia, 3:7-13) and admonishment to others (2:10; 3:14-19). Prediction also forms an important part in these messages to the churches. Smyrna was warned of impending persecution ("you will have tribulation ten days"); in Thyatira the false prophetess Jezebel would be cast on a bed of affliction and go into great tribulation for her wicked deeds; Philadelphia was promised deliverance "from the hour of testing which is about to come upon the whole world" (3:10) and those of the "synagogue of Satan" would be made to bow down at their feet (3:9).

Similarly, Paul miraculously prophesied (predicted) in Acts 27:22-26 that not one life would be lost in the shipwreck on his journey to Rome. Not only did this constitute a marvelous vindication of Paul as God's prophet to the unbelievers who guarded him, but it also comforted and encouraged those who, along with Paul (e.g., Luke who wrote "we" in 27:27, 29), faced the ordeal.

In light of this, whether the information involved elements of prediction or resulted in edification, comfort, or encouragement does not militate against its essence as being the miraculous impartation of revelation to the prophet by the Holy Spirit which, in turn, is proclaimed to members of the Christian community. Therefore, it is unlikely that a proclamation made apart from immediate revelation may strictly be termed "prophecy."

The Ecstatic State of the Prophet

The ecstatic or prophetic state of the prophet also demonstrates the unique revelatory role of the prophet as a spokesperson for the Lord. In the Old Testament, certain stereotyped phrases reveal the prophetic state. For example, "the Holy Spirit entered into" the prophet and that prophet received revelation (e.g., Ezek. 2:2; 8:3; 11:5-12, 24; 12:1), or "the hand of the Lord" was on the prophets when prophetic communication was received (e.g., 3:14, 22; 8:1; 33:22; 37:1). Sometimes the phrase "the Spirit of God came upon" is used to describe the revelatory state (Num. 24:2; 1 Sam. 10:10; 11:6; 19:20; 2 Chron. 15:1; Isa. 61:1), or the phrase "the word of the Lord came to" is used (1 Kings 19:9; 1 Sam. 15:10; 2 Sam. 24:11; Jonah 1:1; Hag. 1:1; 2:1, 20; Zech. 7:1; 8:1). Another phrase is "filled with power, with the Spirit of the Lord" (Mic. 3:8).

New Testament prophets exhibited a similar prophetic state. In the state of ecstasy (e[kstasi") Peter received revelation regarding the inclusion of uncircumcised Gentiles like Cornelius into the fellowship of the church (Acts 10:10; cf. ejkstavsei in 11:15). Paul related that in the ecstatic state (ejkstavsei) he was warned to depart from Jerusalem because of the hostility of the Jews and was commissioned to be an apostle to the Gentiles (22:17; cf. 9:26-30). John was "in the Spirit" on the Lord's day (Rev. 1:10, ejgenovmhn ejn pneuvmati) and because of this prophetic state he was enabled to receive the contents of the Book of Revelation (cf. 4:2, ejgenovmhn ejn pneuvmati; and 17:3 and 21:10, kaiV ajphvnegkevn me ejn pneuvmati). "Through the Spirit" (ejshvmanen diaV tou' pneuvmato") Peter predicted the coming famine during the reign of Claudius (Acts 11:28). In the prophetic state Paul received "visions" (ojptasiva") and "revelations" (ajpokaluvyei") from the Lord (2 Cor. 12:1). Genuine New Testament prophets who were in the prophetic state (ejn pneuvmati qeou') were guarded from erroneous revelatory statements because of the intimate ministry of the Spirit of prophecy (1 Cor. 12:3). The Holy Spirit exercised sovereign control over the true prophet's prophetic activity. These verses also serve to stress the special relationship the Holy Spirit maintains to the prophetic state, which demonstrates the miraculous and rational nature that such experiences entailed for both Old and New Testament prophets.

In summary, prophecy was a Spirit-mediated miraculous gift. Several factors demonstrate this. First, the primary characteristic involved was Spirit-motivated speech centering in direct reception of revelation from God. Without such revelation, prophecy does not function. Second, supernatural discernment, insight, and knowledge were frequently involved in conveying information that could not have been obtained by ordinary human means. Third, prophecy often involved prediction. Prediction was a vital element in biblical prophecy in contrast to secular examples of profhteiva. Fourth, edification is better understood as the effect of prophecy on the listener rather than as its content. Fifth, the Spirit-mediated prophetic state of the prophet reinforced the supernatural element involved. This miraculous element of prophecy is frequently neglected in determining the meaning, nature, and function of the gift.

A Comparison of Prophecy to Related Gifts

A comparison of gifts related to the gift of prophecy is also needed since erroneous equations of the prophetic gift are made because of failure to give due recognition to the miraculous nature of prophecy.

The Prophet and the Teacher

Prophets and teachers are frequently mentioned as the most significant proclaimers of the Word in the church

(Acts 13:1; 1 Cor. 12:28; Eph. 4:11; Rom. 12:6). Like teachers, prophets mediated knowledge, so that one could learn from them (1 Cor. 14:31; Rev. 2:20; cf. Didache 11.10-12). Prophets instructed the church regarding the meaning of Scripture, and through revelations, they gave information about the future.

However, prophecy is not the same as teaching. Because it was based on direct divine revelations, the ministry of the prophet was more spontaneous than that of the teacher. Teachers, on the other hand, preserved and interpreted already existing Christian tradition, including relevant Old Testament passages, the sayings of Jesus, and traditional beliefs of earlier Christian teaching. Furthermore, while the teacher considers the past and gives direction for the present on the basis of what took place or what was said previously, the prophet looked toward the future and guided the path of the believing community forward.

In the New Testament, the presence or absence of revelation distinguishes prophecy from teaching. Prophecy always depended on a revelation from God, but by contrast no human speech act which is called a didachv or didaskaliva ("teaching") done by a didavskalo" ("teacher") or described by the verb didavskw ("to teach") is ever said to be based on ajpokavluyi" ("revelation"). Furthermore, no ajpokavluyi" in the New Testament is ever said to result in a "teaching" of one man to another. Instead, teaching is put in contrast to divine "revelation." Teaching is simply an exposition or application of Scripture (Acts 15:35; 18:11, 25; Rom. 2:20-21; Col. 3:16; Heb. 5:12) or a repetition and explanation of apostolic instruction (Rom. 16:17; 1 Cor. 14:17; 2 Thess. 2:15; 2 Tim. 2:2; 3:10).

The Prophet and the Preacher

Some commentators assert that prophecy is essentially another name for preaching. An example of this is Redpath, who asserts that prophecy "is the gift of the man who in the name of the Lord and in the power of the Spirit is able to speak with authority from the Book to the day in which he lives." MacArthur distinguishes between revelatory prophecy, which has ceased, and prophecy today, which he defines as "the ability to proclaim truth powerfully." Perhaps this association has been built up because of the "forthtelling" aspect in the prophetic activity of the prophet as the spokesman for God.

However, to equate preaching with the spiritual gift of prophecy is fallacious. Such an equation is also quite artificial. While preaching is essentially a merging of the gifts of teaching and exhortation, prophecy has the primary elements of prediction and revelation. As Friedrich notes, "All prophecy rests on revelation, 1 C[or.] 14:30. The prophet does not declare what he has taken from tradition or what he has thought up himself. He declares what has been revealed to him." Friedrich's further comment is relevant: "Whereas teachers expound Scripture, cherish the tradition about Jesus and explain the fundamentals of the catechism, the prophets, not bound by Scripture or tradition, speak to the congregation on the basis of revelations." Therefore, since the preacher is not in contact with God as was the prophet, the preacher is not the modern equivalent of a prophet. While both preacher and prophet proclaim, the reception of direct revelation from God is the crucial essence of the prophetic gift that qualitatively separates it from other forms of proclamation and preaching. Furthermore, while preaching includes teaching, the ministry of the prophet was more spontaneous, being based on direct divine revelation.

The Prophet and the Evangelist

Like the prophet, an evangelist (eujaggelisthv") utilizes proclamation. Similarly, prophecy is not addressed solely to Christians but may also have an evangelistic value for unbelievers (cf. 1 Cor. 14:24-25). This evangelistic value of New Testament prophecy is also seen in its Old Testament counterpart (e.g., Jonah 3:5). Yet important differences in the two gifts mark out their distinctiveness. Evangelism is addressed primarily to unbelievers who have not yet heard or accepted the message concerning Jesus Christ, while prophecy has its primary focus on believers in the congregation (1 Cor. 14:3, 29-37). The content of both gifts must also be distinguished. The evangelist proclaimed the content of the gospel, while prophecy is based on the miraculous impartation of immediate revelation which could not be known through ordinary human means (the "secrets of his heart are disclosed," 1Cor. 14:25).

The Prophet and Knowledge

First Corinthians 13:8-12 deals with prophecy and gnw'si" ("knowledge"). They are similar in that both are charismata of the Spirit, both are concerned with knowledge of mysteries, and both are fragmentary rather than definite or perfect (13:9). In contrast, however, gnw'si" is not superior to prophecy, but prophecy is the supreme gift of grace. Furthermore, they differ in the way the knowledge of mysteries is attained and in the use to which this knowledge is put. Gnw'si" is a rational gift of the Holy Spirit which deals with the ability to grasp the logical nature and relations of truths revealed, whereas prophecy rests on direct revelation. Furthermore, while gnw'si" is individualistic, prophecy is by its very meaning and nature concerned with proclaiming to others.

Arguments for the Cessation of Prophecy

The temporary nature of miraculous gifts as espoused by many cessationists is based on theological deductions made from certain New Testament passages. Though many verses are sometimes used (e.g., Rom. 15:18-19; 2 Cor. 12:12; Rev. 22:18), two prominent passages will be discussed: Ephesians 2:20 (ejpiV tw'/ qemelivw/ tw'n ajpostovlwn kaiV profhtw'n - the foundational nature of New Testament prophecy) and 1 Corinthians 13:10 (o{tan deV e[lqh/ toV tevleion - the temporal nature of New Testament prophecy). The theological argumentation for the cessation of prophecy also is enforced by a comparison of the biblical data regarding prophecy with current practices of so-called "prophecy" exhibited among noncessationist groups. Also in the same way Old Testament prophecy ceased and the canon of the Old Testament was closed, New Testament prophecy reasonably may be considered to have ceased following that same analogy.

Ephesians 2:20

An important verse arguing for the cessation of such gifts as New Testament prophecy is Ephesians 2:20. In verses 19-21 Paul, employing the temple structure as a metaphor to describe the church, distinguished between apostles and prophets on the one hand and individual Christians on the other by relating them to one another as a foundation is related to the walls resting on it (cf. 1 Pet. 2:4-8). Articles two and three in this series have demonstrated that Paul portrayed the apostles and New Testament prophets as comprising the foundation of the church (appositional genitive) with Jesus Christ as the chief Cornerstone. The entire church is said to be built on the foundation of those apostles and prophets and on no one else.

Ephesians 2:20 clearly refers to the universal church, not to some local church or mission field. Paul's predominant usage of ejkklhsiva elsewhere in Ephesians demonstrates this. In 3:5 he wrote that the apostles and prophets were closely related to the foundational revelation that Gentiles, as well as Jews, would be united in the one universal body of Christ (cf. v. 10). He also used this universal sense in 3:21. In 5:23-27 the illustration of the husband and wife shows Christ's relationship to the universal church. This universal church is described as "His body" (v. 30) and also as a mystery (v. 32), referring back to 3:5. Paul's words, therefore, cannot be properly applied to local or national churches throughout this age, inasmuch as Paul's representation of the church throughout this passage and elsewhere describes the church in the most universal and pervasive of terms (e.g., "God's people" and "God's household" in 2:19). Therefore, Paul was referring to the foundation of the universal church in Ephesians 2:20. This foundation, by implication and by its very nature, can be laid only once since foundations are necessarily laid only once at the beginning of any structure.

Ephesians 3:5-10 helps interpret 2:20, for it deals with the revelatory impact the apostles and New Testament prophets had in the church. From 3:5 it becomes clear that apostles and New Testament prophets were of primary importance as vehicles of revelation, thereby providing the foundation for the church: the mystery (musthvrion) of Jewish and Gentile inclusion in the universal body of Christ, the church (3:9-10). This mystery was disclosed to the whole church, not to just a local congregation (1:8-10, 17, 18) through the apostles and prophets, of whom Paul was one (2:20). Paul said this revelation about Gentiles being included in the church had not been made known previously (3:5) but "has now" (wJ" nu'n) been revealed to the apostles and prophets and is contained in canonical revelation (e.g., Ephesians). This mystery was fully revealed to the body of Christ by the end of the apostolic era through proclamation (as evidenced in the Book of Acts and epistles like Ephesians). This first generation laid the foundation through the reception of such revelation. This can be seen by the wJ" nu'n, which contrasts the former age, in which people did not know of Gentile inclusion, with the present time of the writing of Ephesians, and also by the use of the culminative aorist indicative ajpekaluvfqh, signifying the attainment of effort or process. Once that revelation had been made, it no longer needed to be given by the Spirit again since it was proclaimed by the apostles, particularly Paul. Once a mystery is revealed, it is no longer a mystery and does not need to be revealed again.

Furthermore, apostleship in Ephesians 2:20 must correspond to a narrow definition, being restricted to first-century apostles, especially since this verse is related to the apostles of 3:5-10 and the mystery of Gentile inclusion in the church is no longer being revealed. The direct relationship of 3:5-10 with 2:20 makes it most likely that the apostles mentioned in 2:20 were those commissioned directly by Christ, who received such important revelations (Acts 10; 2 Cor. 12:1-2; Gal. 1:11-12) and were the primary instruments in the spread of the gospel in the first century (to the Jews, Acts 2; to the Samaritans, Acts 8; to the Gentiles, Acts 10; and as far as Rome in the case of Paul, Acts 13-28). The term qemevlio" ("foundation") is a key term, for the foundation was obviously established during the first century when apostles, as eyewitnesses of Christ's ministry and commissioned by Him, were still alive (cf. 1 Cor. 9:1-2; 15:8; 2 Cor. 12:12).

Moreover, the prophetic gift was closely associated with the gift of apostleship. Prophets are found alongside apostles in the New Testament as playing a special role in laying the foundation (Eph. 2:20) and in receiving revelation (1 Cor. 12:28; Eph. 2:20; 3:5; 4:11; Rev. 18:20). This close association of the two gifts is verified by the Didache, Ignatius, and the Muratorian Fragment. To second-century writers, apostleship was a thing of the past. If the first century marked the end of the apostolic gift, it is probable that it marked the end of the prophetic gift also.

Since Paul was referring to the universal church in Ephesians 2:20 and the apostles and prophets laid the church's foundation by receiving and transmitting revelation (3:5), the strong implication is that once the church was established, the gift would be discontinued. By its very nature, a foundation cannot be continuously relaid. This verse clearly implies that Paul viewed revelation as occurring during a specific, nonrepeatable era, with the church of subsequent ages commanded to discover its foundation in those apostles and prophets, or more specifically, in their doctrine as it is recorded in the Scriptures. Since the passage labels prophecy in itself as a foundational gift, the inevitable conclusion is that New Testament prophecy ceased along with the gift of apostleship.

The major objection to this reasoning is that it is a theological deduction from the text and not something the passage explicitly states. Mallone argues, "The intention of this verse is not to say that these gifts have ceased but only that a gift exercised must be in harmony with the instruction of the founding apostles and prophets." In reply, it has already been demonstrated that Ephesians 2:20 signifies that the foundation consists of the apostles and prophets (appositional genitive) and does not refer to their teaching activities (subjective genitive). Since they are the foundation, the building illustration clearly seems to indicate the idea of the cessation of such gifts. While it is true that all teaching and instruction must be in harmony with that of the apostles and prophets, the central thrust of the illustration is the foundational role of such individuals in the church's formation and, as such, would indicate the temporary character of such offices by the very nature of the illustration. As already noted, once the foundation has been laid by the apostles and prophets of the first century it does not need repeated formation by others.

Some may respond by saying that perhaps the definitions of apostle and prophet are too restricted, and that other apostles and prophets may be a part of the superstructure besides those referred to by Paul here in Ephesians. True, apostleship can have both a general and a limited meaning. In a general sense, the word ajpovstolo" ("apostle") means "one who is sent" (from ajpostevllw, "to send"), or "a messenger." The Latin term is equivalent to the word "missionary." Hence in a general sense every Christian is a missionary or an apostle, because he has been sent into this world to render a testimony for Christ. Epaphroditus illustrates this idea, for the word "apostle" is used of him (Phil. 2:25).

However, in the specialized sense of the gift of apostleship, the word ajpovstolo" refers to the office of apostleship (Acts 1:20-26). Paul apparently had this specialized sense in mind in Ephesians 2:20. The apostles, like Paul and the Twelve, were a distinct group far different from those designated by any general usage of the term. The first-century apostles and New Testament prophets received special revelations and participated in the foundation (qemevlio") of the church (Eph. 3:5). Once that foundation had been laid by those in the first century who possessed the gifts of apostleship and prophecy, no further need to relay the foundation by subsequent generations is implied. Therefore, no ground exists for seeing need for any further apostles and prophets since they have fulfilled their primary purpose and the church builds on that foundation as Ephesians 2:20 naturally implies. The burden of proof for seeing a general class of apostles and prophets continuing in the superstructure must rest on those asserting that such a class exists today. Furthermore, such contentions go far beyond the purpose of Paul's illustration in the context and rest on tenuous definitions.

First Corinthians 13:8-13

Much of the controversy surrounding spiritual gifts, particularly the miraculous gifts like prophecy, tongues, and knowledge, has concentrated on 1 Corinthians 13:8-13 as providing a crux interpretum regarding the continuance or cessation of the gift. Both sides have centered on this passage to argue either for or against the cessation of the prophetic gift.

All groups would agree that 1 Corinthians 13:10 indicates that gifts such as prophecy, tongues, and knowledge are temporary. That such gifts will cease is not at issue so much as when those gifts will cease and what particular time is being indicated by the phrase o{tan deV e[lqh/ toV tevleion in 13:10. Whenever toV tevleion arrives, then these gifts will no longer be necessary. While the analyses of the passage have produced a variety of interpretations, the major views essentially reduce to two possible ways of rendering toV tevleion.

The first view understands toV tevleion in an absolute sense of "perfect" and has reference to Christ's Parousia. Here the significance of toV tevleion is identified as "the perfection" that will exist after Christ returns for His church, as seen in 13:12. At that time, all spiritual gifts, not just prophecy, and knowledge, will cease. The only virtue which has permanent significance is love (v. 13).

Several arguments are advanced in favor of this view. First, this view is the only one that adequately satisfies the explanatory confirmation of 13:12 where the ideal, final state is in view. Second, the meaning of "perfect" best describes the period after Christ's return. Third, the verb e[lqh/ can refer only to the precise moment of Christ's second coming. Fourth, Pauline statements of eschatological hope center in Christ's return (1 Cor. 1:7-9; 15:20-34; 1 Thess. 4:13-18). Fifth, Paul and other New Testament writers used the related term, tevlo", of the same period (Rom. 8:18-30; 1 Cor. 1:8; 15:24; Matt. 24:6, 13-14). Sixth, maturity and the end are related in Paul's writings (Col. 1:5, 22, 27-28).

The second view is that toV tevleion refers to what is "mature" or "complete" rather than "the perfect state." Understood in this sense, toV tevleion draws on the figure of the church as Christ's body collectively growing up during the age since the day of Pentecost. The gifts of 1 Corinthians 13:8-9 gradually ceased with the close of canonical revelation and the increasing maturity of the body of Christ (cf. Eph. 4:11-16, esp. v. 13, eij" a[ndra tevleion, "the mature man").

Admittedly any decision on these two options is not easy. However, the second view ("maturity") is the more viable. Arguments for the second view also constitute a rebuttal of the first view. First, Pauline usage of tevleio" never conveys the idea of absolute perfection, and such a philosophical meaning is also questionable in the rest of the New Testament. Only this view allows tevleio" a relative sense. Second, Paul's constant use of the nhvpio" . . . tevleio" antithesis supports this interpretation. Tevleio" elsewhere always possesses a relative meaning of "mature" when used in proximity to nhvpio" (13:11, o{te h[mhn nhvpio", "when I was a child"; cf. 1 Cor. 2:6; 3:1; 14:20; Eph. 4:13-14). Furthermore, the occurrence of tevleio" is what suggests the nhvpio"illustration of 1 Cor. 13:11 (cf. Heb. 5:13-14). Whenever the adjective is used in connection with nhvpio", it always carries the connotation of gradual increase, not of an abrupt change. Third, this view gives an adequate sense to the illustrations of 1 Corinthians 13:11 and 12. In verse 11 a relative maturity is signified, while verse 12 indicates an absolute maturity. Provision also exists here for the ultimate state after the Parousia, according to the demands of verse 12, in that maturity is of two kinds: one that is constantly changing and increasing (v. 11), and the other that is final and absolute (v. 12). The latter type is viewed in 13:12 as a future goal.

Fourth, Ephesians 4:13-14 more explicitly presents the picture of the maturing of Christ's body collectively. A number of striking resemblances between 1 Corinthians 13 and Ephesians 4 tie these passages together in reference to gradual maturity. The parallels between these two passages are strengthened also by the historical connection of the writing of 1 Corinthians while Paul was ministering at Ephesus (1 Cor. 16:8). Since Ephesians 4:13-14 pictures a gradual development of Christ's body from the beginning to the end, Paul's picture in 1 Corinthians 13 would also convey the same concept. Fifth, this view provides for Paul's uncertainty as to the time of the Parousia and status of a written canon. Sixth, as already suggested in note 69, the contrast with ejk mevrou" in 13:9 requires a quantitative idea ("complete") rather than a qualitative idea ("perfect").

In light of this, Paul's development from childhood to adulthood in verse 11 illustrates the progressive growth of the church through the critical period of its history. Ultimate maturity is another matter, as is illustrated in verse 12 when growth reaches its culmination at Christ's return. Thus, this view is comprehensive enough to embrace the relative maturity implied by the illustration in verse 11 as well as the absolute maturity depicted in verse 12. It pictures believers collectively growing up together in one body, beginning with the birth of the church on the day of Pentecost. The body of Christ attains different states of maturity during this period until complete maturity is reached at the Second Coming of Christ. The contrast in verse 13a is that gifts of the earlier part of the paragraph were possibly to extend only through a portion of the church's existence, whereas faith, hope, and love would characterize the entire earthly ministry. Beyond this, only one of the three virtues will survive the Parousia, and that is love itself. For this reason, it is declared to be the greatest gift. As Thomas concludes,

"When the mature comes" gathers together into one concept both the period of church history after the need for the gifts of direct revelation has ceased to exist (relative maturity illustrated in v. 11) and the period after the return of Christ for the church (absolute maturity illustrated in v. 12). By comparing these gifts to the maturity of the body of Christ Paul shows their temporary character (in contrast with love). A certain level of maturity has been reached once the N.T. canon has been completed and is in hand, and so the result is almost the same as that of [the completion of the New Testament canon view]. Yet Paul expected an imminent return of Christ and could not know, humanly speaking, that there ever would be a complete N.T. canon of 27 books before Christ returned. Hence, he was guided by the Spirit to use the more general language of maturity to allow for this.

Thus, the gift of prophecy, along with tongues and knowledge, was a temporary gift which is no longer operative today.

The Argument from the Revelatory and Miraculous Nature of Prophecy

Much regarding this argument has already been hinted at in the discussion above and in this series as a whole. Current attempts at prophecy parallel one of the flaws displayed in the second-century heresy known as Montanism: the phenomenon of false prophesying. False prophesying was a strategic reason why the church soundly rejected Montanism's claims of being a genuine "prophetic" movement. Accordingly, the New Testament (Acts 2:17-21) and the post-apostolic early church saw a fundamental continuity, not discontinuity, between Old and New Testament prophets and prophecy. Therefore, false prophesying still remains one of the key signals for detecting false prophets.

As this study has shown, according to both the Old and New Testaments the miraculous nature of genuine biblical prophets and prophecy is that true prophets are one-hundred percent correct in all that they prophesy. Either a prophet was always and completely accurate or he was to be rejected as a false prophet.

Stress also must be given to another often-neglected axiom of Scripture. Even if the prophecy of a so-called "prophet" comes true, no guarantee exists that such an individual is a true prophet, for even false prophets are capable of occasional true prophecies and "signs" or "wonders" (Deut. 13:2). While true prophets always prophesied accurately, false prophets sometimes prophesied accurately. The inaccuracy of the false prophets' prophesying constituted them as false prophets. Hence constant vigilance is required (1 Cor. 14:29-31). Prophets must be closely scrutinized. Any prophet who even once prophesied falsely was to be rejected summarily by God's people. "The prophet who shall speak a word presumptuously in My name which I have not commanded him to speak . . . that prophet shall die" (Deut. 18:20). Proponents of the current practice of "prophecy" attempt to assert that Old Testament commands no longer apply to present-day "prophets." However, as has been demonstrated in this series of articles, no evidence exists that the apostles, who were Jews steeped in the Old Testament, ever thought that such Old Testament requirements were substantially modified or abrogated in judging prophets. As stated in the second article in this series, Paul's warning in 1 Corinthians 14:29-31 to judge prophecies is a direct development from such Old Testament warnings and also corresponds to Jesus' warnings against false prophets who will try to deceive God's elect by false signs (Matt. 7:15-16; 24:11, 24; Mark 13:22; 1 John 4:1; cf. Hos. 4:6). Constant vigilance and careful examination by God's people are required in dealing with prophets who prophesy falsely or who exhibit false "signs" and "wonders."

Geisler identifies a crucial issue regarding fallible prophets.

Many today claim to be receiving visions, dreams, and revelations from God. The problem is that their "revelations" are not infallible. Some of them are flatly wrong. But a fallible revelation from God is a contradiction in terms. . . .

The problem with making testable prophecies in the name of the Lord is that they might prove to be false. This might not seem to be too significant until we remember that the test of a prophet is not whether he is sometimes right but whether he is ever wrong. Moses declared, "If what a prophet proclaims in the name of the Lord does not take place or come true, that is a message the Lord has not spoken. That prophet has spoken presumptuously" (Deuteronomy 18:22). The penalty for false prophecy under the Old Testament law was death (v. 20). If that law were still in effect today, there would undoubtedly be far fewer persons claiming prophetic powers.

Several other recent works have also cataloged false prophecies by modern-day charismatic proponents who assert that the gift of prophecy is still active.

Anyone claiming the prophetic gift today must be scrutinized in light of the nature of the gift as revealed in the New Testament. Those who assert such activity must be subject to the regulations set forth in Scripture. By claiming the prophetic gift, they are asserting that they have direct contact with Jesus Christ, which is nonnormative and unique among the rest of the members of the body of Christ. Prophecy involves a miraculous impartation of revelatory information not known on a mere human basis. This is further substantiated by the fact that the New Testament prophetic gift involved much more than teaching, preaching, evangelism, or the possession of certain kinds of knowledge. While these latter activities may be accomplished on a purely human level, the New Testament prophetic gift was a miraculous and supernatural revelatory gift that differed antithetically from what may be accomplished by naturalistic means. Because of the miraculous nature of prophecy, current novel attempts at defining prophecy have also impugned the basic substance of prophecy. That is, nothing miraculous exists in a gift that is conceptualized to include the possibility of "mistaken" prophecy whereby the prophet is sometimes accurate and sometimes not. Even modern fortune-tellers can claim varying degrees of partial or intermittent accuracy. However, genuine biblical prophets and prophecy are qualitatively different from any such novel practices. Recent attempts at redefining prophecy are directly contrary to its essential nature as a miraculous gift. Grudem, whose book constitutes the mainstay of defense for the Vineyard movement's approach to "prophecy," directly admits that Vineyard prophets can be and are mistaken at times. "Prophecy in ordinary New Testament churches was not equal to Scripture in authority but was simply a very human-sometimes partially mistaken-report of something the Holy Spirit brought to someone's mind."

Any prophetic pronouncements must stand the test of accuracy and uniqueness found in such places as Deuteronomy 13:1-5; 18:20-22; 1 Corinthians 14:28-32; and 1 John 4:1-3. The moment that a prophetic pronouncement demonstrates itself as being inaccurate or wrong, then such prophecy must be labeled as a false prophecy given by a false prophet. It would seem reasonable to contend that no person today who would presently claim the prophetic gift could ever make claims to such an absolutely perfect record of supernatural and miraculous accuracy which is required of true biblical prophets. Indeed, a close examination would reveal an overwhelming trend to a great level of inaccuracy. If persons claiming prophetic status are evaluated on the basis of a correct understanding of the biblical data and requirements for prophets, the light Scripture sheds on such activity demonstrate that the genuine gift of prophecy has ceased.

The Argument from the Analogy of the End of Old Testament Prophecy

As noted in the second article in this series, Judaism as a whole in the time of Jesus held that prophecy had ceased since the time of Malachi. Though there were claims to prophetic activity (as in, e.g., the Essene community of Qumran), such claims need to be distinguished from genuine prophecy in terms of canonical recognition and general Jewish acceptance. Early Christians also knew the opinion of Judaism on this issue. If they viewed Old Testament prophecy as having ended, then it is reasonable that they also entertained the same possibility for New Testament prophecy.

Grudem attempts to escape this conclusion by his definitional bifurcation of the gift. He distinguishes between canonical revelation of the apostles and an alleged form of edifying prophecy in 1 Corinthians 12-14. He contends that because such prophets "mistakenly" misunderstood the nature of the prophetic gift as speaking the "actual words of God," which was reserved for apostolic prophets, they were eventually rejected by the church. However, as noted previously, Grudem's dichotomizing here is highly tenuous. Such distinctions in prophetic authority have been shown to be unsound. Contrary to Grudem, church history reveals that a rise of false prophecy led to the outright rejection of those claiming the prophetic gift, as especially evidenced in the church's decisive repudiation of Montanism. The first-century church and post-apostolic church applied Old Testament standards to judge New Testament prophets and prophecy. Hence in light of the analogy of the end of Old Testament prophecy, the church increasingly emphasized the close of the New Testament canon as that canon was recognized.

Conclusion

From the nature of the discussion in this series, the evidence demands the view that the New Testament prophetic gift ceased its operation very early in the history of the church. Furthermore, although no one single argument alone demonstrates this, the aggregate weight of the total evidence decisively points to this conclusion. When claims to prophetic activity today (and indeed throughout church history) are compared to the biblical record, woeful inaccuracy and inadequacy of such practices are evidenced. If the data from Scripture regarding the nature and practice of the biblical gift of prophecy and the testimony of church history are used as the standard to judge claims of the present possession of the gift of prophecy, the Vineyard movement's practice of prophecy and the prophetic practices of "charismatic" groups as a whole show the need for the body of Christ to reject soundly such claims. It is of paramount importance to make a diligent, careful scrutiny of the scriptural evidence regarding such activities. Only by such a close examination can the body of Christ guard against serious doctrinal error and misunderstanding which can and does result from such concepts of "mistaken" prophecy. The sincerity of those claiming the prophetic gift today is not called into question by this series. However, the support for such claims is what is called into serious doubt and is completely rejected. When such an examination is conducted, contemporary claims are rendered entirely suspect.

Christ's warning to His church must be heeded: "Beware of the false prophets . . . You will know them by their fruits" (Matt. 7:15-16a; cf. 24:11, 24; Mark 13:22; Acts 20:28-31). While the cessationist camp arguably may have "survived" the tongues issue of previous years, this Vineyard and charismatic concept of a form of "mistaken" or fallible prophets and prophecy that is sweeping across traditional lines has the potential of doing untold harm to God's people (Jude 3).

Other Books By This Author

BIBLICAL CRITICISM

BEYOND THE BASICS

Edward D. Andrews, F. David Farnell, Thomas Howe, Thomas Marshall, Dianna Newman

www.ingramcontent.com/pod-product-compliance
Lightning Source LLC
Chambersburg PA
CBHW061333040426
42444CB00011B/2904